M★O★R★E
GREAT
INTERVIEWS

M★O★R★E
GREAT
INTERVIEWS

JOHN CLARKE

A Rathdowne Book
Allen & Unwin

© John Clarke 1992

This book is copyrighted under the Berne Convention. No reproduction without permission. All rights reserved.

First published 1992

A Rathdowne Book
Allen & Unwin Pty Ltd
9 Atchison Street, St Leonards, NSW, 2065

10 9 8 7 6 5 4 3 2

National Library of Australia
Cataloguing-in-Publication

Clarke, John 1948-
    More great interviews.
    ISBN 1 83673 268 3.
    1.Australian wit and humor. I. Title II. Title: Current Affair (Television program).
A823.303

Cover design by Mark Davis
Front cover image courtesy The Nine Network
Text designed by P.A.G.E. Pty Ltd, South Melbourne, VIC 3205

Printed by Australian Print Group, Maryborough, VIC 3465

Contents

THE HON. PAUL KEATING, TREASURER
The Banking Inquiry   1

THE HON. PAUL KEATING, TREASURER
On Government and Business   4

THE HON. PAUL KEATING, TREASURER
The Crossword   7

THE HON. PAUL KEATING, CELEBRATED BACKBENCHER
Resting Between Engagements   10

THE HON. GARETH EVANS, MINISTER FOR FOREIGN AFFAIRS
The Great Leap Sideways   14

THE HON. R J HAWKE, PRIME MINISTER
Attracting the Green Vote   17

THE HON. R J HAWKE, PRIME MINISTER
Religious Instruction   20

THE HON. CHARLES BLUNT, LEADER OF THE NATIONAL PARTY
Trouble with Stamps   23

A BHP SPOKESMAN
Protecting the Environment   26

THE HON. JOHN HEWSON, LEADER OF THE LIBERAL PARTY
On the Waterfront   29

THE HON. R J HAWKE, PRIME MINISTER
A Standing Ovation   32

SENATOR BOB COLLINS, MINISTER FOR SHIPPING
The Front Fell Off   35

THE HON. JOHN HEWSON, LEADER OF THE LIBERAL PARTY
Consumption Tax   39

THE HON. PAUL KEATING, CELEBRATED BACKBENCHER, PREVIOUSLY WORLD'S GREATEST TREASURER
I'd Rather Not Discuss It   42

MR CHRISTOPHER SKASE, ORNAMENT TO AUSTRALIAN BUSINESS
A Message from Spain   45

THE HON. PAUL KEATING, CELEBRATED BACKBENCHER, PREVIOUSLY WORLD'S GREATEST TREASURER
A Plea for Compassion   48

SIR JOH BJELKE-PETERSEN, PREMIER OF QUEENSLAND (1725-1987), ACCUSED OF CORRUPTION. TRIED. FOREMEN OF JURY REVEALED AS SUPPORTER. JURY DISMISSED. LEGAL SYSTEM GIVEN BYE THROUGH TO NEXT ROUND.
Trial Buy Jury   51

SENATOR GRAHAM RICHARDSON, MINISTER FOR VARIOUS THINGS AND PARTY NUMBERS MAN (BLACK BELT, BAR AND CLASP)
On His Support for the Hawke Prime Ministership   54

SENATOR GARETH EVANS, MINISTER FOR FOREIGN AFFAIRS
Peace in Our Time   57

THE HON. JOHN HEWSON, LEADER OF THE LIBERAL PARTY
Explaining the Tax Package   60

THE HON. R J HAWKE, PRIME MINISTER
A Christmas Message   63

A PRIMATE OF THE CHURCH
On the Ordination of Women   66

MR R J HAWKE, RECENTLY RETIRED PRIME MINISTER
Responding to Suggestions that His Resignation
Lacked Dignity   69

MR R J HAWKE, '60 MINUTES' INTERVIEWER
A Reversal of Roles   72

SENATOR KIM BEAZLEY, MINISTER FOR EDUCATION
The Clever Country   75

A NEWSPAPER EDITOR, 46, OF SYDNEY
A Matter of Principle   78

MR PETER WALSH, EX-SENATOR AND FINANCE MINISTER
The View from Outside the Compound   81

DR TERRY METHERELL, EX-MINISTER IN THE NSW GREINER GOVERNMENT. RESIGNED FROM MINISTRY BUT RETAINED SEAT ON PROMISE OF EXECUTIVE POSITION WITH ENVIRONMENT PROTECTION AUTHORITY.
The Selection Process   84

THE HON. NICK GREINER, PREMIER OF NEW SOUTH WALES
Safeguards for the Public   87

SENATOR GRAHAM RICHARDSON, MINISTER FOR ALL SORTS OF THINGS AND FAMILY MAN
A Storm Brewing   90

A MAFIA SPOKESPERSON
On Gang Warfare   93

DR TERRY METHERELL, EX-MINISTER IN THE NSW GREINER GOVERNMENT
Dear Laws of Evidence   96

MR ALAN BOND, RETIRED YACHTSMAN
An Investment Opportunity   99

THE HON. BARRY JONES, CHAIRMAN OF THE AUSTRALIAN LABOR PARTY
Parent-Teacher Night   102

THE HON. JOHN DAWKINS, TREASURER
The Great Communicator   105

THE HON. PAUL KEATING, PRIME MINISTER
Women on Stamps   109

THE HON. JOHN HEWSON, LEADER OF THE LIBERAL PARTY
Rapping with the Duds   112

THE HON. PAUL KEATING, PRIME MINISTER
Is There Any Point?   115

THE AUSTRALIAN OLYMPIC COACH, LIVE FROM BARCELONA
Prospects for the Competition   118

THE AUSTRALIAN OLYMPIC COACH, LIVE FROM BARCELONA
The Position After the First Week   121

MR BRIAN GREY, EX-CHIEF EXECUTIVE OF COMPASS AIRLINES
Checking the Overhead Locker   124

THE HON. JOHN HEWSON, LEADER OF THE LIBERAL PARTY
The New Zealand Experiment   127

THE HON. PAUL KEATING, PRIME MINISTER
A Policy Vindicated   130

THE HON. NORMAN LAMONT, CHANCELLOR OF THE EXCHEQUER
The Currency Crisis   133

A TOAST

Bryan Dawe and I began doing these interviews in 1989 and before that we worked together on radio. It is a very amusing privilege to work with someone whose understanding of speech rhythms is supernatural, who is an unerring judge of character and who considers a day without mischief a wasted day.

I would like you all now to charge your glasses please. Ladies and gentlemen, I give you, Bryan Dawe.

Thank you.

THE HON. PAUL KEATING, TREASURER

The Banking Inquiry

Mr Keating, thanks for joining us again.
Thank you; always a pleasure.

The inquiry you've announced into the banks, what's it for?
Well, we deregulated the Australian financial sector completely a few years ago.

How did you do that?
We took away the regulations that were governing the behaviour of the banks and the lending institutions.

Yes, why did you do that?
Well, that's what we're going to find out.

Mr Keating, the fact that you're having an inquiry indicates that what you expected hasn't happened. What did you expect?
We expected that there would be a great deal more competition in banking and that this would keep interest rates down and build a firm capital base for Australian industry.

And what was the result?
Well there isn't any Australian industry and of course there's no need for a firm capital base, because there's no competition and interest rates are far too high.

What happened?

The banks, which ought to have made a lot of money, paradoxically made catastrophic losses, and we're going to have an inquiry into the whole matter.

So every element of the plan has gone wrong?

Frankly, it's not looking good for the plan; I think the smart money's against the plan at this stage.

So was there any way of predicting that this would happen before it occurred?

The only way to determine that this might happen would have been a great deal of research and a great deal of deep analysis.

And you did that?

No, that's what we're going to do starting next Tuesday.

Any other inquiries?

We're going to look into insider trading.

What's that?

Insider trading is a very interesting idea; apparently people use special knowledge that no one else has got to get a firm advantage for themselves and make a great deal of money which no one else has got the opportunity to get.

Unlike banking.

Unlike banking.

That's a very interesting idea, isn't it?

We're also going to look into the tooth fairy.

The who?

The tooth fairy. You know the tooth fairy, when your tooth comes out, and you put it under the pillow?

Yes of course.

Well, we're looking into the matter of the tooth fairy. Apparently at the moment it looks as if there is no tooth fairy.

Well…how does it happen?
Apparently it's your parents.

I'm sorry?
Apparently it is your parents—there is no tooth fairy. It's not as if the tooth fairy's just unavailable because he's doing someone else's choppers, there *is no* tooth fairy.

No tooth fairy; it's extraordinary.
Want to know how we found this out?

Well, I was going to ask you that.
The Stork told us.

Oh right. Mr Keating, thanks for joining us.
It's nearly time for my tablet, if we could finish soon I'd be grateful.

We have finished.
Have we? Good.

**THE HON. PAUL KEATING
TREASURER**

On Government and Business

Mr Keating, thanks for joining us.
Thank you, it's a pleasure.

You've had a pretty high-profile time in Parliament lately. You're about the only one left standing.
I haven't had a bad week, frankly, beating back the dingbats.

Do you think Mr Hawke will give evidence at the Royal Commission in Western Australia?
I don't know.

He's been invited.
He's been invited, yes, but I think you'll find he's washing his hair; he didn't look all that anxious to me.

Do you think you overreacted by pointing out that John Howard and Fred Chaney had had dealings with Laurie Connell?
No, I don't think so, you see that's a material point. They can't get up and accuse the other side of having a connection with Laurie Connell when some of their own more significant primates have got a connection with Laurie Connell. They can't do that.

But isn't this just guilt by association?
No, the question is one of consistent argument. You can't accuse somebody else of something you're doing yourself. That's hypocrisy.

Yes, but doesn't this mean that any political party that's had a hundred grand slung at it by Laurie Connell appears as if it's done something wrong?
In Australia?

Yes.
I shouldn't think so. How many parties are there who haven't had a hundred grand slung at them by Laurie Connell in recent years?

The Democrats.
But they're not going to get into power, are they?

Why not?
Because they can't run a proper election campaign.

Why not?
Because they haven't got enough money.

Why not?
Look, Laurie Connell can't fund everything in the whole country, can he? The man's doing what he can; he's obviously only got so much money. He can't fund the entire democratic process!

Mr Keating, on another matter, how did you react to the economic indicators during the week?
Oh, they were pretty good.

Could you be more specific?
They were VERY good. How specific do you want me to be?

In what sense were they good?
There are a couple of small businesses still running in South Australia, but by and large we're on track.

Isn't there an engineering plant in Queensland?

I shouldn't think so; doing what?

Exporting parts for harvesters.

What's a harvester?

It's a thing that cuts wheat.

Sheaves.

I'm sorry?

Sheaves. It sheaves the wheat off and sheaves it up into sheaves.

Does it?

Yes. I don't know why, but that's what they do.

Well, it's making a lot of money apparently.

Look, I didn't say we were perfect, I didn't say we'd eliminated all commercial activity, I simply said the economy was on track. That's all I said.

Mr Keating, thanks.

I made no other claim.

Mr Keating, thanks.

Don't thank me, son, we'll get to you. Are you under contract, are you?

I think so.

We'll get you, you'll be under 'C'. You'll be sheaved some time in the next fortnight.

THE HON. PAUL KEATING, TREASURER

The Crossword

Mr Keating, thanks for coming in by the way, we'll be off in a minute.
That's no trouble at all.

How's the leadership challenge going?
Oh, don't mention it. Very bad week for the leadership challenge.

What's wrong?
Well, Bob got up and announced that we'll have inflation down to four per cent within the life of the current parliament.

What are you going to do?
Might have to shoot the current parliament, I think. How am I going to get inflation down to four per cent? It's not possible.

Why did he predict it?
Because he knows I can't do it.

So, you look like an idiot, and he stays in charge?
Yes.

(looks at crossword) **What's this: 'Economy completely destroyed'.**
'Economy completely destroyed'? What's it begin with?

R-E-C.
Recovery?

No, it's got a double 's' in it.
Double 's'? In the middle?

Yep.
Messiah.

What?
Messiah?

No, it's...recessio?
Recessio? Yes, Handel's Recessio.

What's that?
It's a brand of suit isn't it?

I wasn't sure. So do you think you'll challenge Bob when you get the numbers?
I've got the numbers now.

Oh.
Eleven down is 'Hawke' incidentally.

No, I got that.
You got it? What is it?

'Sphincter'.
Oh.

If you've got the numbers, why don't you go now?
Well, I've got the numbers in Cabinet but no one else wants me.

Oh. I thought nobody wanted him?
Nobody does want him, but they want him more than they want me.

That's why he's so popular.
Yes, he's cunning isn't he?

(referring to crossword) **Ah, 'Politician'?**
'Politician'? I'll get this. How many letters?

Four.
Four? Four-letter word meaning politician. Four letters?

I can't think of anything.
I can think of something.

What?
Mm?

What?
I'm not going to say it on this network till after about 11.30.

Oh.

THE HON. PAUL KEATING, CELEBRATED BACKBENCHER

Resting Between Engagements

Mr Keating, thanks for joining us.
Well it's a very great pleasure to come in, and thank you for inviting me.

It's very much appreciated.
It's really no trouble whatever, it's good to be back. How've you been?

Oh terrific, yourself?
Good thanks.

You've had a lot quieter week this week.
Been a bit quiet, yeah.

What do you actually do up there on the back bench?
Oh well, there's plenty to do. I'm halfway through *Anne of Green Gables*; I've filled in the 'O's in the *Fin Review* by about 10.30.

Have you been watching the performance of the Prime Minister?
Oh look, I don't want to be drawn into any comment about the performance of the Prime Minister. I had a go and I was beaten. It was a good fight, a swift fight, a fair fight. I got beaten, that's it.

When are you going to have another go?
I'm not going to have another go.

Oh come on.
I'm not going to have another go.

Come on, Paul, please.
I'm *not* going to have another go. Especially not…

August the fifteenth?
…Who told you about the August the…Who said that?

Listen if you did have another go, do you think you'd win?
On August the fifteenth?

Yes.
It's not going to happen.

Put it this way. If the Prime Minister went and you were carried by acclamation, would you accept it then?
On August the fifteenth?

Yes.
Probably not, no.

If he did resign and you were carried by acclamation, who'd be in your cabinet?
On August the fifteenth?

Yeah.
I've got no idea.

Well who was going to be in your cabinet on Monday, if you'd won?
Well, obviously the people who'd supported me.

And who were they?
Well, clearly, from the group who supported me would be drawn the personnel who would have made up a Keating front bench in the event that I had won that ballot.

Yes, and who were they?
Well, obviously: Paul Lyneham for foreign affairs, Laurie Oakes for industry, Alan Ramsey, Kerry O'Brien, Michelle Grattan.

What would she do?
Well, we were going to get up a chair in objective journalism at ANU, she could get that.

And what would it be called?
The Paul Keating Chair in Objective Journalism. She could have got it.

What do you make of the beat-up this week with Senator Walsh and the phone-tapping business?
Oh hang about, that's a very serious story.

I'm sorry.
Very serious story.

What did you think of that very serious story this week about Senator Walsh and the phone-tapping?
In 1927?

Yes.
I was very impressed with the prompt action Senator Walsh had taken, and if I were Billy Hughes I'd do something about it.

There's been a huge sell-off of the Australian dollar today; what would you have done if you'd remained Treasurer?
August the fifteenth.

Pardon?
Oh I'm sorry, what was the question?

August the fifteenth?
No that was the answer, what was the question?

When are you not going to mount another challenge?
Not going to mount another challenge?

Yes.

August the fifteenth.

So, the Prime Minister's fine on August the fifteenth?

Oh absolutely. No challenge whatever on August the fifteenth. None whatever.

Mr Keating, thanks for joining us.

Thank you very much.

See you again.

Yes, August the fifteenth.

**THE HON. GARETH EVANS,
MINISTER FOR FOREIGN AFFAIRS**

The Great Leap Sideways

Senator Evans, thanks for coming in.
It's always a pleasure, thank you.

I wonder if I could ask you about the lifting of sanctions in South Africa...
Yes, I wonder if you could.

...I'd like to; who's behind it?
The international community is behind it.

Could you be more specific?
The very rich, perhaps slightly more white elements in the international community are behind it.

What's Australia's attitude?
Well, we're pretending to be a rich country and of course we've pretended for a very long time to be a white country.

So we're going along with it?
Well, we're not opposed to it.

**President Bush says, and I quote, 'Significant advances have now been made in dismantling apartheid, and gradual easing of sanctions is appropriate now that these improvements are beginning to take effect.' How does he gauge something like this?

He doesn't. He recognises that there's going to be a feeding frenzy, and he wants to be in for his chop.

What about Switzerland when it says that the ultimate effect of sanctions is that it's the blacks who suffer? What does it mean?

It means that they're going to make so much money out of trading international currencies when the lights go green that you would require oxygen if I were to mention even part of what they're going to be taking out of the place in one day.

Senator Evans, why is Japan going to lift sanctions at the end of the month?

Oh, concern for the black community, I would think. The record of Japan in fighting racism has been very, very good for quite some time now.

Since when?

Well, it's been excellent since Wednesday.

So who was *against* lifting the sanctions?

Oh, only the blacks, really.

And what's been done about that?

There have been a lot of conferences. I think the international community's very anxious that the blacks be party to the process whereby over a sustained period of time...

Yes I understand that. Are there many blacks in South Africa?

Oh yes, the majority of the population of South Africa is black.

Well, why don't the sanctions stay in place?

They didn't impose the sanctions; they're not the Government, and they're certainly not the international community.

So who did the international community impose sanctions on?

On the white South African Government.

So they were opposed to the South African Government?

No they weren't, they're white too. You see, the international community has to be very careful not to be seen to be taking sides.

So, more blacks down holes digging up diamonds?

Well, some of them will be down holes looking for diamonds, but a lot of them won't; a lot of them will be down mines looking for fruit...

So this looks like a...

...down mines looking for wheat. Down mines looking for anything.

...like an exciting period...

...a lot of them will just be down mines...

...an exciting period for democracy in South Africa?

Oh absolutely, yes.

THE HON. R J HAWKE, PRIME MINISTER

Attracting the Green Vote

Mr Hawke, thanks for joining us.
Thank you, it's a pleasure to be here.

Could I ask you about your environmental policy?
Environmental policy? What environmental policy?

Well, the one you announced before the election.
Oh, the one about the trees? That was an electoral policy, I know the one you mean. What about it?

Why have you abandoned it?
We haven't abandoned it at all.

Oh Mr Hawke…
We haven't abandoned it. Don't yell at me! Don't even think of yelling at me! Do *not* even think about it.

Mr Hawke, I'm only asking…
Do not even entertain the prospect of yelling at me!

Mr Hawke, I'm not yelling at you.
I'm sick of these environmentalists. Are you an environmentalist?

I've been trying to express myself on this all week; the only thing about these wilderness areas is there's going to be a little bit of mining in the middle of it. Nothing round the outside. Just a road, some fast-food joints and a bit of a mess in the middle. Bit of noise pollution, but it won't worry you if you don't live within a couple of hundred thousand miles.

All right, Mr Hawke, if you haven't abandoned it will you reaffirm it?

Of course we'll reaffirm it.

When?

We've got a very big announcement being made in months to come.

When?

On March the fifteenth of next year.

And when is the election?

I've no idea when the election is.

Well, approximately.

Approximately March the sixteenth.

The following day?

The following day, technically. If you've got a problem, if you think that's cynical, we can announce it on the fourteenth, or the eleventh, or the tenth. It simply doesn't matter. We're deeply, *deeply* committed to the environment, and the trees and all that stuff.

Would you think of announcing it after the election?

Not much point in announcing your environmental policy if you're not in government, son.

Are you saying you may not be re-elected?

I don't know son. I don't know if we're going to win the election— we only won the last election because Graham Richardson found an environmental policy down the back of the piano at half past six on the Friday. I don't know!

Do you seriously think the environmentalists are going to believe you this time?
I don't know. They're a very, very cynical group and they don't believe a great deal. They didn't believe us last time, and they don't believe us now. You can't win with these people.

Well, you can't win without them.
You what?

You can't win without them.
You *are* an environmentalist, aren't you? Have you been to a university?

Yes I have.
I knew you had.

Mr Hawke…
Now don't yell at me, don't yell at me!

I'm not yelling at you!
Don't yell at me!

Mr Hawke, thanks for joining us.
Stop yelling at me.

I'm not yelling at you.
You are yelling at me!

I'm not yelling at you.
Do *not* yell at me. I have told you before not to yell at me.

Mr Hawke, thanks for joining us.
STOP YELLING AT ME!

**THE HON. R J HAWKE,
PRIME MINISTER**

Religious Instruction

Mr Hawke, thanks for joining us.
Thank you for inviting me.

You gave Archbishop Hollingworth a caning this week.
Oh, I don't know that I gave him a caning.

Mr Hawke, you gave him a caning.
Well look, the man has to understand to stay out of the economic debate. He's an archbishop; it's all very well for him to favour us with a few noble observations, but he should stay out of the debate. I'm not running an ideal world, I'm running a real economy, in a real country, in the real world.

But surely, Mr Hawke, he has the right to criticise an apparent shortcoming in government policy?
I didn't say he doesn't have the right to do that. I said he doesn't know what he's talking about. He knows absolutely nothing about economics.

Do you have to be an economist to have an opinion about the way the country's being run?
Well obviously you've got to know something about economics if you're going to make statements that bear on the economic debate. If you don't, your comments are going to be irrelevant. Now the archbishop's were, and I took the liberty of pointing that out to him.

But if your economics program can't accommodate a basic level of caring for the people that live here, surely the policy must be changed. That's what he was arguing.

Does anybody disagree with that? That's just a rhetorical statement. Do we need an archbishop to point that out to us? Frankly, I don't need a lecture about Christian ethics. I grew up with the Christian morality, I frankly don't need it described to me. Who was it for instance, in this country, who got up and promised to get rid of child poverty? Who was that?

Mr Hawke, it hasn't happened.

It hasn't happened yet.

You said it was going to happen by the beginning of this year.

It hasn't happened by the beginning of this year yet.

But Mr Hawke…

Who was it—let me finish—who was it who got up in this country and quite openly wept, quite openly wept for the massacre of the innocents in Tiananmen Square? Was that the archbishop?

That was you.

That was me. Who was it who *again* quite openly got up, and confessed *freely* to having fooled around with other women and hopped into the turps slightly as a younger man? Was that the archbishop?

The archbishop probably wasn't unfaithful to his wife.

Well is that my fault? Am I to be crucified because some archbishop didn't monkey about with other women?

Mr Hawke, I'm sorry I doubted you.

Are you happy?

(sotto voce) **Yeah.**

If it's all right with you, I think I'll go.

OK.

Open the door.

(door opens to thunderous Hallelujah Chorus)
Have you got any bread and perhaps a bit of fish?

Surely to God you're not going to try and feed all them out there?
No, of course not.

What are you going to do?
I'm going to make myself a sandwich, I haven't had any lunch.

**THE HON. CHARLES BLUNT,
LEADER OF THE NATIONAL PARTY**

Trouble with Stamps

Mr Blunt, I wonder if I could ask you a few questions if you wouldn't mind?
Yes, by all means. Make yourself at home, sit down.

You seem to be in the news a bit today.
Yes, I was distressed to see that, I haven't done anything wrong, I don't know what all the fuss is about.

Mr Blunt, I was wondering, why did you spend two hundred and fifty-five thousand dollars on postal charges in the two weeks leading up to the election?
Well, I went down to the post office to post a letter.

And what happened then?
The post office was shut; if they left the post office open normal hours it wouldn't have happened.

So what happened?
Well, the post office was shut.

So what did you do?
I had to use the coin-operated stamp vending machine. Have you ever tried to use one of those?

No.

Well, I put forty-one cents in, and a stamp came out. You have to pull it out, and I just tried to tug it slightly, and it ripped off. So I got half a stamp.

And what happened then?

Well, I put another forty-one cents in and I got a full stamp, but it went down to halfway down the second stamp. So I got a half of one stamp and half another stamp with a perforation down the middle, so I stuck another forty-one cents in.

Why didn't you take the top of one stamp and put it on the bottom of another stamp?

Because I thought the problem might with be the forty-one cent stamp, so I started putting different money in and ordering different stamps. And I couldn't make the stamps match up and I couldn't make the picture fit. See you can't make a West Australian wildflower meet with the top half of a boat. Some of them have got yachts on, and I got another one with a koala, and I couldn't make it fit with a cricketer.

What happened in the end?

Eventually I got a forty-one cent stamp, put it on the letter, posted the letter.

What did that cost?

To post a letter?

Yes.

Hundred and twenty grand.

But that doesn't explain the other hundred and forty five thousand dollars.

We export! This is the country's lifeblood, we export stuff all the time!

What do you export?

Well, we export cattle for instance.

Cattle? You export cattle?

Big exporter of cattle here.

You export cattle in postage bags?

I exported two hundred shorthorn bulls to Dusseldorf on Monday.

In the mail?

They were there on Wednesday. *In* the marketplace, on Wednesday. Takes six weeks if you send them on the boat. Why would you do that? This country's got to wake up.

Are there any other things you send in the post?

My wife went on holiday with the children for three weeks.

What's that got to do with postage charges?

I posted them.

Mr Blunt, I've got to go, could you order me a taxi?

Where are you going? I'll post you. Are you going back into town?

Yes.

(calling to an assistant) Get a bag, Cheryl!

A BHP SPOKESMAN

Protecting the Environment

Thanks for joining us.

Thank you very much for inviting me in Jana, it's a very great pleasure to be here.

No, I'm sorry, I'm not Jana.

Oh I'm sorry, I'm in the wrong place. *(gets up to leave)*

No, no, this is 'A Current Affair', I'm not Jana.

Oh I see. Well thank you very much for inviting me in, Notjana, it's a great pleasure.

Fine. You're having a dispute with Greenpeace over your exploration off the coast.

Well yes, there is some ground between us left to cover. The precise detail you see of what we're doing seismically is somewhat at odds with the general principles espoused by Greenpeace, general principles, I might say, which we also espouse, general principles the espousal of which would be axiomatic, I would think, to any understanding of environmental issues.

Yes. Could you be more specific?

Yes, we were going to dig a dirty great hole in the seabed because there's a quid in it, and we got caught and we're rather embarrassed about it.

What does Greenpeace say is wrong with what you're doing?
They say the area we want to dig up is a whale-breeding area.

Is it?
No, it's not.

It isn't?
No. Well, that is to say, it won't be.

When won't it be?
It won't be when the whales get out of the area, will it?

Where are the whales going to go?
I don't know, I don't even know that there are any whales there.

Isn't it a breeding ground, though?
I've never seen any whales breeding out there.

Well have you been out there?
Of course I've been out there, I was out there the other day.

On a whale-spotting boat?
No, on a dirty great big new drilling rig we've got that can displace an area the size of India in an hour and a half. Fantastic thing.

And there were no whales breeding?
I didn't see any.

Did you hear any?
I beg your pardon?

Where are they going to breed then?
I don't know, but I can tell you something, they don't breed in the sea out there.

Where other than the sea out there do you think whales breed?

I don't know about whale-breeding. I'm not making myself clear: dirty great big holes in the seabed I can do for you; knowledge about whales I don't have. I'll tell you something about your whale: he's not a moron. The whale is a highly intelligent critter, I've seen them go through hoops at Seaworld. Your whale's got enough brain to get out of the area while we're drilling, for goodness sake.

Can I put it another way? Is there oil out there under the sea bed?

We don't know but we currently think so.

Have you got shares in BHP? Are you a shareholder?

Yes, of course I am.

Have you got shares in whales?

No, you can't get shares in whales son. You don't buy shares in whales. Horses: yes, whales: no. I've got a share in a horse.

And how do you get a return from that?

They breed. You breed them. Why would you breed a whale? Your whale's got no speed and he can't stay; he's no good over hurdles your whale, and he's useless on the flat.

Thanks for joining us.

Have you ever backed a whale? I can't remember when I've ever backed a whale.

We're out of time, I'm sorry.

You'll get decent odds son, but keep your money in your pocket.

**THE HON. JOHN HEWSON,
LEADER OF THE LIBERAL PARTY**

On the Waterfront

Dr Hewson, thank you for coming in.
Thank you for inviting me.

Support for the Coalition parties is sixteen percentage points above that of the Government.
Yes, support for the conservative parties at the moment is very high indeed.

And your popularity is up, as well.
My personal popularity is breathtaking.

You must be very pleased with this.
I'm a very pleased person. I'm delirious with happiness.

And why do you think this is?
Well, because we've got a good team, and good solid, strong, derisive leadership.

Decisive.
I beg your pardon?

Decisive.
Who is?

You are.

Who says?

The polls.

Are you serious? What, I'm considered a good leader in Poland?

No, no, here, in the popularity polls.

Oh, in Australia? I'm sorry.

What are you going to do? Are you going to make some announcements, stir things up a bit?

Oh no, I'm not going to *say* anything, I wouldn't say anything.

Why on earth not?

My popularity will go down if I say anything. That's been the pattern. I've only got one advantage: I'm not Bob Hawke. That's why I'm popular. If I say anything, my popularity goes down. I announced that we were sending the troops into the wharves and my popularity went down. I can't afford to say anything.

If we could talk about that: you were going to send in the army?

Well, aerial bombardment first, obviously, but then send in the army, yes.

You were going to run bombing raids?

High-level bombing raids, yes, just to soften them up before we send the troops in. Before the ground war starts you've got to soften the enemy up.

And what about nuclear weapons?

Well, I wouldn't rule them out. This is a very serious position.

You would seriously think about nuking Australian waterfronts?

Well, I think we might have to; this is a very serious business. Do you realise that in Singapore they can turn a ship round in five hours? Five hours to turn a ship completely round!

And how long do we take?

In Australia?

Yes.
It'll be four years on Saturday.

Do you think there'll be any collateral damage here?
Well, we may lose a Peter Reith or two, but I don't think anything serious will happen.

Why Peter Reith?
Well, because we say he's an essential aspect of the future plan of course.

And what do they say?
They think he's a milk treatment plant.

And what is he in actuality?
In actuality he's a decoy, we get them made up in Switzerland. They're very good, they look like a Peter Reith, they sound like a Peter Reith, they've got the same thickness as a Peter Reith which is…

…fairly thick.
Fairly extreme. But they're not a fully operational Peter Reith. Have you ever seen Peter Reith?

Yes, of course.
Fully inflated?

I don't think I've seen him any other way.
Well, we've got cupboards full of them.

Is that right?
Yeah. If something goes wrong we get another one of them. You can see the join if you know what you're looking for.

And what are you looking for?
Somebody to replace Peter Reith.

**THE HON. R J HAWKE,
PRIME MINISTER**

A Standing Ovation

Mr Hawke, thank you for coming in.
Thank you for inviting me in.

The Hobart conference seems to have gone very well.
Fabulous success, standing ovation I got; they all got on their feet and ovated, right at me.

What did you do?
I just stood and generally acquiesced in their fulsome approval of my many qualities—it was a healing time for the party.

Did they all clap?
Oh yes.

Did Peter Walsh clap?
Well, no, he can't, but everyone who could clap did clap.

How did the Barry Jones decision this week help that healing process?
I'd like to say something about Barry Jones if I may. He's a very remarkable fellow. He it was who warned ten years ago that we had no manufacturing basis in this country and that the sunrise new technology industries gave us an excellent opportunity to get one. He it also was who first warned of the greenhouse effect. He's a very remarkable Australian.

Did we get any of those new technological industries?
No, but the countries who listened to Barry Jones did.

What countries?
Well, like Wales, for instance.

Wales?
Yes, Wales has got the silicon valley industry for half Europe.

Why didn't *we* listen to Barry Jones?
Because he was the Minister for Science and Technology. Nobody listens to the Minister for Science and Technology.

Why not?
Very junior ministry. He's got no numbers at all, the Minister for Science and Technology.

So how did Mr Jones help with this healing of the wounds within the Party?
By standing aside for a dumber man.

Mr Hawke, why did the conference avoid the issue of uranium?
It didn't, we had a debate about that yesterday.

Mr Hawke, you decided not to change the policy.
Yes, but only after a very full and passionate debate.

I didn't see that at the conference.
No, it was in John Bannon's bathroom. A couple of number-crunchers from the Left had a TKO over a couple of people from the mining lobby.

And what did you do at the conference?
I just did a medley of my hits.

Which ones?
Oh, I did 'Australia you beauty I love this country it's a fabulous place', I did 'I promised the party I'd stay on till the next election and by God I will'.

Did you do that bit where you get Hazel up and you raise her arm?
Oh, the triumph bit? Yeah, never fails.

It works?
Absolutely never fails with an audience, that one.

And what are you going to do now?
Well, you get up and clap now.

I what?
You stand and applaud.

Here?
Yeah, in a spontaneous manner. Just move into it and clap.

Clap? *(starts clapping)*
Hands above the head I think. Bravo; a few bravos.

(clapping) **Bravo! Bravo!**
Can these people clap? Lot of people here, can they all have a go? *(all begin clapping, calling 'bravo!')*

That's the sort of thing, yeah. *(calls offscreen)* **Hazel! Hazel! Well go and get her. Somebody go and get her. Yeah, that's it, keep it going.**

**SENATOR BOB COLLINS,
MINISTER FOR SHIPPING**

The Front Fell Off

Senator Collins, thanks for coming in.
It's a great pleasure, thank you.

This ship that was involved in the incident off Western Australia this week...
The one the front fell off? That's not very typical, I'd like to make that point.

How is it untypical?
Well, there are a lot of these ships going round the world all the time, and very seldom does this happen. I just don't want people thinking that tankers aren't safe.

Is this tanker safe?
Well, I was thinking more about the other ones.

The ones that are safe?
Yes. The ones the front doesn't fall off.

If this tanker isn't safe, why did it have eighty thousand tonnes of oil in it?
I'm not saying it wasn't safe, it's just perhaps not quite as safe as some of the other ones.

Why?

Well, some of them are built so the front doesn't fall off at all.

Wasn't this one built so that the front doesn't fall off?

Obviously not.

How do you know?

Because the front fell off, and twenty thousand tonnes of crude oil spilt and the sea caught fire. It's a bit of a giveaway. I'd just like to make the point that that is *not* normal.

What sort of standard are these sea tankers built to?

Oh, very rigorous maritime engineering standards.

What sort of thing?

Well, the front's not supposed to fall off for a start.

And what other things?

There are regulations governing the materials they can be made of.

What materials?

Well, cardboard's out.

And?

No cardboard derivatives.

Paper?

No paper. No string, no Sellotape.

Rubber?

No, rubber's out. They've got to have a steering wheel. There's a minimum crew requirement.

What's the minimum crew?

Oh—one I suppose.

So the allegation that they're just designed to carry as much oil as possible and to hell with the consequences, that's ludicrous is it?

Absolutely ludicrous. These are very, very strong vessels.

So what happened in this case?
Well, the front fell off in this case, by all means. but it's very unusual.

But Senator Collins, why did the front fall off?
A wave hit it.

A wave hit it?
A wave hit the ship.

Is that unusual?
Oh yes. At sea? Chance in a million!

So what do you do to protect the environment in cases like this?
Well, the ship was towed outside the environment.

Into another environment.
No, no, it's been towed beyond the environment. It's not in the environment.

No, from one environment to another environment.
No, it's beyond the environment—it's not in an environment, it's been towed beyond the environment.

What's out there?
Nothing's out there.

There must be something out there.
Look, there's nothing out there—all there is is sea, and birds, and fish.

And?
And twenty thousand tonnes of crude oil.

And what else?
And a fire.

And anything else?
And the part of the ship that the front fell off. But there's nothing else out there.

Senator Collins, thanks for joining us.
It's a complete void.

Yes. We're out of time.
The environment's perfectly safe. We're out of time? Can you book me a cab?

But didn't you come in a Commonwealth car?
Well yes, I did.

What happened?
The front fell off.

**THE HON. JOHN HEWSON,
LEADER OF THE LIBERAL PARTY**

Consumption Tax

Dr Hewson, thank you for joining us.
It was the very least I could do; it would be very difficult to interview me if I hadn't.

Of course. You seem to be very close to an announcement of your consumption tax policy.
Oh, we're just a whisker away now, I think it could happen any day.

You nearly announced it this week, didn't you?
I came perilously close to almost saying something sensible on Wednesday, yes.

Why didn't you announce it then?
Well, there are one or two details still to go in.

What can they possibly be? Haven't you been working on it since the war?
Actually, it's not the tax we're worrying about; the tax is now formulated.

What's the problem then?
The problem is how we sell it to people.

What's the problem with selling it to people?
Well, I think there's a suspicion one or two people might see

through it.

Why is that?
Some of them can count, apparently.

Isn't that a good thing?
An ability with numbers is…yes, I should think, normally an excellent thing, but it's not much use to you if you're going to try and sell a consumption tax.

Why's that?
Because it's supposed to be fair and reasonable. A flat consumption tax applies to all goods and services and therefore appears to be equal and equitable.

Yes, it applies to wealthy and poor alike.
That's the theory. But of course in practice it applies to the poor alike.

Why?
Because it only taxes the part of your income you spend on consumption. It doesn't tax anything you save or anything you invest. If you spend all your income it's a tax on a hundred per cent of your income, any fool can see that.

It's been very successful in New Zealand, hasn't it?
I don't know about that. Who told you that?

Well the Americans who bought New Zealand Telecom were very impressed.
Get away.

What exactly happened over there?
Well, what they did in New Zealand was introduce a ten per cent across-the-board goods and services tax.

At what rate?
At the normal rate.

What's that?
What's the normal rate for a ten per cent tax?

Yes, what is it?
Twelve-and-a-half per cent.

Did the economy come good in the end?
Well, a bit early to say at the moment. I think the vet's still in there—it's not looking all that good, frankly. I think it's still on a drip.

Dr Hewson, what are you going to do?
I'm going to keep burbling on about it, because it's party policy to keep talking about it all the time.

How are you going to do that?
I'm condemned to it—I'm going to talk about how fair and reasonable and equitable it is, how it *sounds* fair and reasonable and equitable.

And hope they don't notice.
And hope no one notices.

Do you think they'll notice?
They won't if you shut up about it.

I won't say a word.
I'm not saying anything to a soul.

I won't say a thing.
I haven't said a sausage.

Dr Hewson, thanks for joining us.
Sssh.

OK.

**THE HON. PAUL KEATING,
CELEBRATED BACKBENCHER,
PREVIOUSLY WORLD'S GREATEST
TREASURER**

I'd Rather Not Discuss It

Mr Keating, thanks for coming in.
Well, thank you for inviting me in.

Lovely to see you again.
It's great to be back, thank you very much.

I wondered if I could ask about the figures that were released this week.
The inflation figures? The June quarter inflation figures?

Yes, and the unemployment figures.
The ten per cent?

Yes.
Coupled with the twenty-eight per cent figure for teenage unemployment?

Yes.
Not to mention the hundreds of thousands of people who don't even bother to register.

Yes.

And neither to mention the financial burden of having seven hundred thousand people on the dole.

Yes.

And to say nothing of the fact that men are falling out of the workforce at a rate higher than that of women.

Yes.

Because you don't have to pay women so much. So you get a deregulated labour market.

Yes.

And you've got a hundred thousand new migrants coming in every year.

Yes.

Just to swell the figure.

Yes.

Well, what about interest rates? Would you like to talk about that?

Yes.

Which they're refusing to lower?

Yes.

In case they imperil the economic miracle?

Yes.

And what about the American wheat sales? You want to talk about that?

Yes.

Which are robbing us of our two major markets?

Yes.

Which they said they'd never do because they're totally opposed to any form of regulation or centralised planning in an economy?

Yes.

In fact they're pretending to be totally in favour of free trade and open competition?

Yes.

And while they're also pretending to be our friends?

Yes.

In fact, whenever they want anything, Bob's got to bend over quick as look at you, for his pal George?

Yes.

'Here are three ships George and I think it's your putt?'

Yes, yes.

And why we've got no opposition in Canberra at all?

Yes.

First sign of anything wrong in the current account and you've Peter Reith coming out on to the Parliament steps and giving us another demonstration of his accent?

Yes.

'I've been to all the right schools, I just can't remember why'?

Yes.

No, I don't want to talk about any of that.

Why not?

I caused it.

**MR CHRISTOPHER SKASE,
ORNAMENT TO AUSTRALIAN BUSINESS**

A Message from Spain

Mr Skase, thanks for coming into the studio.
I'm not in the studio in any financial way; I'm only here to talk to you. I've got no involvement with it.

Are you coming back to Australia?
I'd very much like to come back there. I remember Australia very fondly of course, I have photographs of it all over the house.

Where are you living at the moment?
Well, you know those tumbledown old mission houses you often find near the industrial waste section of some of the older European cities?

Sure.
Well, I live in a four-hundred room house overlooking that.

And how do you live?
Very nicely thank you.

No, I mean how do you pay for it all?
I'd like to thank the Australian taxpayer while I have the opportunity; I haven't run up a formal speech and I haven't spoken

about the matter for some time, but I understand there's a recession back there and this is absolutely fantastic over here. This is beyond my expectations.

What sort of general day do you have over there?
Well, take today—got up around 10, 10.30, a little crushed orange juice out on the terrace, wandered down to the exquisite little town. They just pull the garfish straight up out of the sea, pop them on the burner. A standard handful of that and you're ready for coffee. And then I normally slip under a sun umbrella and have a little kip with the *Guardian Weekly* over my face for forty.

What's the time there now?
It's just about opening time here now.

What, you're going for a drink?
No, the banks are nearly open; nearly time for the banks to open.

What do you do down there at the banks?
Well, a few of the boys and I go down to the banks for a laugh in the morning. We have a bit of a laugh over here, it's very funny.

Mr Skase, what about this inquiry back here? Will you be coming back to answer questions?
Well, not immediately. I can't travel unfortunately at the moment.

Why not?
I'm having laser treatment for a bad back.

What exactly is the problem with your back?
I don't know yet, the bloke with the laser's not here.

You mean he's actually going to *give* you a back problem?
Well we think it'll be a back problem; you can get a leg problem and as a matter of fact I had my name down for a corked thigh at one stage, but we think we'll go for the back.

Do you intend to come back here to answer questions at any point?
Do I intend to leave this country which has no extradition arrange-

ment with Australia and come back there and answer a lot of questions from a barrister in the witness box about where the two hundred million went?

Yes.

Oh yes, absolutely, soon as possible. Soon as the back clears up.

Well, when might that be?

Just a minute, excuse me, the bank's opened... *(aside)* Pardon? Well just send someone down there to laugh, tell them I'll be there shortly, I'll just see this guy off.

When will you be coming back?

Is Bob Hawke still the Prime Minister there?

Yes, he is.

He's not, is he? Still? Who's the opposition?

The Liberals.

Ha ha! You're joking! Really? *(aside)* Get a deposit slip, you can still do it.

Mr Skase, satellite time's running out, thanks for joining us.

I'm not joining you, son.

**THE HON. PAUL KEATING,
CELEBRATED BACKBENCHER,
PREVIOUSLY WORLD'S GREATEST
TREASURER**

A Plea for Compassion

Mr Keating, thanks for joining us.
Thank you for inviting me in.

You've had some pretty damning things to say this week about the performance of the Government.
Well, I've just been fulfilling a few speaking engagements I promised I'd do a while ago.

How many?
About fifteen or sixteen a day.

You don't see this as an attempt to destabilise the Government in any way?
I'm a member of the Government, why would I do that?

What are you saying?
I'm saying that the country is being destroyed by the economic policies of the Government in the past six weeks.

Just the past six weeks?
A million people are unemployed in this country at the moment; think about what that means. One million people have got no job, no wage, no income...

Yes, but Mr Keating, where did all this unemployment come from?
The policies of the last six weeks.

Mr Keating, you were the Treasurer for the past eight years.
I was. It took me eight years to get the economy of this country to stand on its pedestal and six weeks later it's gone.

Well what are you suggesting be done about it?
We've got to decide what a government is in this country; a government *is* the people in a democracy. We've got to support one another. It's time for compassion, is what I'm saying.

Well, what can the Government do about the unemployed?
We've obviously got to create about a half a million jobs.

Yes, but how are you going to pay for it?
Think about what you've just said. Is the camera on me?

Yes.
Is the camera on me right now?

Yes.
I want you to think very carefully about what you've just said. *(weightily)* I'm telling you that one million Australians have got *no* work. And you want to know if we can pay for a solution.

But can we afford to do it, is what I'm asking.
Is the camera on me?

Yes.
(even more weightily) Can we afford *not* to, is my question. And I'm only talking about the registered unemployed. A lot of people don't register, they don't show up in the unemployment figures.

What sort of people?
Women; blacks.

Are you a feminist, Mr Keating?
I am a fairly radical feminist, yes, no point in hiding it. Why should

I hide it? Is the camera on me?

Yes.

(eyes flicking between interviewer and camera) Fifty per cent of the people in this country are women. What chance do women have in this country? Let me ask you what chance do women have? Have you seen the education system in this country?

But Mr Keating, what are you suggesting?

We need a new education system.

What will that cost?

To hell with what it costs! Where are we going to get in this country if all we can think about is money? This is ridiculous, look at the position with blacks. Now I'm not going to tell you, I'm not going to sit here and tell you, that I'm a full-blood Koori; I'm not a full-blood Koori. But for heaven's sake. Children...

Well, what about children?

Is the camera on me?

Yes.

Babies, many of them, very small, tiny, doe-eyed, innocent...

Yes but Mr Keating...

...wonderful, helpless, darling little babies...

But Mr Keating, what should we be doing about them?

Ice-cream, in my view. Possibly jelly.

What did you do with these issues when you were Treasurer?

I created a bold new society in this country and that's something I'm very, very proud of.

What have you been doing in the last six weeks then?

Well, as I say, I think I've worked out how to fix it.

Mr Keating, thanks for joining us.

Thank you.

SIR JOH BJELKE-PETERSEN, PREMIER OF QUEENSLAND (1725-1987), ACCUSED OF CORRUPTION. TRIED. FOREMAN OF JURY REVEALED AS SUPPORTER. JURY DISMISSED. LEGAL SYSTEM GIVEN BYE THROUGH TO NEXT ROUND.

Trial Buy Jury

Sir Joh, thanks for joining us.
It's a pleasure.

You must be very happy that the last few weeks are over.
Well, I was acquitted, that's obviously very comforting. I've been vindicated. Everything I said about the matter has been proven true.

Well, you weren't acquitted actually…
Yes, I was.

No, you got off, Sir Joh.
No, I was acquitted; *acquit*, from the Latin 'acquit', meaning to acquit.

No, the prosecutor just decided not to pursue the matter.
Yes, because he thought I was innocent presumably.

But did he actually tell you you were innocent?
He didn't need to tell me I was innocent. I knew very well I was innocent.

Well why was he prosecuting you if he thought you were innocent?

I don't know, he looked a bit confused from where I was sitting. I think the whole thing was a fiasco.

Sir Joh, I've got his statement here and he didn't say you were innocent at all.

Well, he did let me go, can we agree about that? Are you prepared to concede that?

Yes, Sir Joh, but he didn't say you were innocent.

Well what did he say, if you're so intelliging, intelligong.

Intelligent.

What else did he say?

He said you were too old.

Don't be ridiculous. Why would you fail to prosecute someone simply because he was too old?

That's what he said.

I wasn't in there for my speedo-reading, was I? I was tried for perjury and I got off.

Because you were too old.

Well, in that case I could knock over a very big bank in the middle of Brisbane because I'm too old to prosecute. I'll do the mail train between Mackay and Rockie on Tuesday, I'm too old to get prosecuted according to you.

You'll get caught. You're too well-known.

I'm too old to prosecute, I'm a free man.

Will you take your son?

Of course I will.

Why?

He's too young to prosecute.

But my point is, Sir Joh, that nowhere does the prosecutor say that

you were innocent, or that you were acquitted.

Just because I am too old doesn't alter the fact that I am completely innocent of all these ridiculous charges.

Sir Joh, thanks for coming in.

You can't have a law if you can get away with breaking it by being old. That's just a mockery.

Thanks for coming in.

(drawing gun) Thank you, and put your hands up in the air where I can see them and don't move. *(to an accomplice)* Go through his pockets.

(an accomplice goes through the interviewer's jacket) **Sir Joh, you can't be serious.**

I'm deadly serious, give us all your money immediately. *(throwing a grey wig to his accomplice)* Put a grey wig on. You'll need to look old or somebody might think it's a robbery.

Sir Joh, you're on national television.

I'm far too old to be prosecuted. *(to accomplice)* Here, hold this cane, I'll go and get the car. *(to interviewer)* We're very old, you're not being robbed.

**SENATOR GRAHAM RICHARDSON,
MINISTER FOR VARIOUS THINGS AND
PARTY NUMBERS MAN (BLACK BELT,
BAR AND CLASP)**

On His Support for the Hawke Prime Ministership

Senator Richardson, thanks for joining us, I wonder if could ask…

Well hang on a minute, I didn't say I'd joined you. I expressed an interest in what you're doing, in broad terms, and I approve of what you're doing, and I oppose your opposition. I didn't say I'd join you though, we're not ready for that.

Sure, sure. I wonder if…

Let's see how we go.

I wonder if I could ask you a few questions about what the Government is doing at the moment.

By all means; what we're doing is addressing the unemployment problem, obviously.

How are you going about doing that?

We're trying to get him a job.

Who?

Paul Keating. We actually think we've got him a job, but we're not sure the numbers are there yet.

Paul Keating?

I second that, I'd just like to…oh, I'm sorry, that's part of the question?

I'm talking about the unemployed.

Well, he's not completely unemployed. He's addressing a lot of dinner functions and he's expressing his passionate commitment to the rights of his fellow diners. He's not completely unemployed.

Is this the biggest problem we have here? Paul Keating's job?

Oh yes. We're the Government—if there were a bigger problem, we'd know about it. Have you read the papers? It's the only thing in the papers, we haven't got time to think of anything else. Certainly the biggest problem confronting this country, Paul Keating's job.

What about the ten per cent unemployed across the country?

Oh he'll fix that, that's why we want him in the job.

Paul Keating will?

I'd like to second that…oh, I beg your pardon, he'll do what?

What about youth unemployment—thirty per cent.

Thirty per cent?

Yes.

Youth unemployment?

Yes.

That's not a bad working base, they can move on the employed with thirty per cent, they've probably got the numbers. Tell them to get in touch with me.

What, the unemployed mount a leadership challenge against the employed?

Yes, you tell them to get in touch with me. We'll bang a few swedes together round the back of the bike sheds and beat the mongrels up.

Senator Richardson, we've got a government whose main concern

seems to be an ego battle between two people who caused the problem they're now pretending to solve.

Grossly unfair, and I think you'll find it's libellous, I'm certainly pleased I didn't say that. I support the Prime Minister.

Do you think it's the calibre of the persons in parliament or the system that's wrong?

I support the Prime Minister. Write that down—I support the Prime Minister. Totally.

I mean, in *principle* I'm talking about here.

In what?

Principle.

Well, I'm in the New South Wales Right. You'll obviously have to give that to me in numbers.

Thanks for joining us.

No, you've misunderstood me; I've expressed a commitment to trying to support a broad spectrum interest. I certainly don't think I'm with you. I'm not against you, incidentally. I'm not *quite* sure I'm with you. Do you support the Prime Minister?

Thanks for joining us.

Whoever the Prime Minister might be, at a given moment?

I'm not sure I'm with you.

(looking around) Is that the mood of the meeting?

**SENATOR GARETH EVANS,
MINISTER FOR FOREIGN AFFAIRS**

Peace in Our Time

Senator Evans, thanks for coming in.
Thank you very much, it's a great pleasure to be here.

I'd like to talk about the events that took place this week in East Timor.
Well yes, technically speaking of course it's not East Timor. It's part of Indonesia.

Well, a number of Timorese people were killed this week by the Indonesian Army. What is Australia's attitude to this question?
Well, let me go back a bit. When Indonesia liberated the freedom-loving people of East Timor in 1975, Australia of course was led by Gough Whitlam.

Who was later sacked.
Who was later sacked, indeed, although not quite as badly as East Timor was.

And what did Australia do?
We watched developments very closely and immediately did nothing.

We did nothing at all?
We did nothing at all. We did it immediately and we remained dedicated to an eloquence which I think can only flow from

lengthy periods of complete silence.

How did this affect the military takeover?
Of a very small and relatively powerless East Timor by the biggest standing army in Asia?

Yes.
It went ahead as if absolutely nothing had happened.

A fair reading of the position.
As it happened, yes, an uncanny reading of our attitude at that time.

What have we done since?
Since then, we've remained completely consistent with the determinations made steadfastly and with the highest possible motivation at that time.

We've continued not to do anything?
I wouldn't have put it like that.

How would you put it?
I wouldn't put it at all. I'm a member of the Australian Government. Our policy is not to put anything at all at any time.

If you had to put it, how would you put it?
Well, I would say we've remained completely consistent with the central tenets of an arrangement going back over a period of time and we've made a measured and very carefully-worded response.

We've done nothing?
It's a lot more carefully-worded than that.

How carefully worded?
Look, there are 180 million Indonesians—how carefully-worded do you want it to be?

So we don't do anything.
We are with the central Asian island republics in the sense of a

commonality of purpose *(interviewer packs up and leaves)* in the theatre of central Asian economic and political development. And if we're going to talk about the current position up there, by which I...*(interviewer leaves studio)*...there is a position which one could quite sensibly submit which suggests that these ideas are felt more keenly perhaps in Jakarta even than they are here, in Fantasyland. *(looking around)* Where on earth has everybody gone?

**THE HON. JOHN HEWSON,
LEADER OF THE LIBERAL PARTY**

Explaining the Tax Package

Dr Hewson, thanks for coming in.
Thank you very much for inviting me in.

How's the tax package going?
Selling like hot cakes. I haven't had this much fun since I took my aunty to the pictures. It's going very well, thank you.

Are people falling for it?
Are what?

Are people falling for it?
I think that could have been a little more happily phrased.

Well, let me put it another way. Has anyone spotted the hole in the argument yet?
Look, we're not going to get anywhere here son are we, if you persist in the notion that I'm trying to pull some kind of swiftie. This is a very well worked-out tax package. Wiser heads than yours have been engaged on the creation of this.

Dr Hewson, what is the philosophy behind the package?
To reform the tax system so that investment monies can be directed

into productive enterprise and so that the income tax system can be made fairer.

Make the income tax system fairer?
Yes, so the middle to low income-earners have more money in the hand.

So, a person with an income of twenty thousand a year—will their income tax go down?
Yes, by four point eight per cent.

Someone earning thirty thousand?
Yes it will, by six point eight per cent.

So the more you earn, the more tax relief you're going to get?
Are you getting these figures out of our tax policy?

Yes I am. What about someone who's earning seventy-five thousand dollars a year?
Will their income tax go down?

Yes.
Yes, by I don't know how many per cent.

Guess.
About eight per cent.

Guess again.
Ten?

Up.
Twelve?

Warmer.
Don't tell me fifteen per cent.

Fifteen per cent.
Good Lord.

Dr Hewson, why have you cut out the single-parent benefit for people whose children are over twelve?

Well, obviously we're very concerned about single-parent families. We think they need help. Let's take a single mother: she goes to work, finishes work at the coal mine, child comes home from school, lets itself in. Mother goes to her second job, perhaps as a barmaid, child gets something to eat. Mother finishes that job and perhaps goes on to a job as a cleaner.

Why has she got a third job?

Well, she needs a third job.

Why?

To pay for any medical expenses incurred as a result of the second job.

What's the child doing while she's cleaning?

Gone to bed. It's two o'clock in the morning. Children can go to bed you know; it's a relatively simple exercise.

Dr Hewson, how are you helping single parents?

She's getting a fifteen per cent tax break—the woman's on seventy-five grand a year!

Dr Hewson, single mothers don't earn seventy-five thousand dollars a year.

Oh, there are always exceptions. You can't legislate for exceptions. Are you a single mother? Be frank with me.

Well I'm not, obviously.

Don't see your point. Don't see your point.

Dr Hewson, thanks for joining us.

Pick, pick, pick, pick. It was going bloody well till I came in here.

**THE HON. R J HAWKE,
PRIME MINISTER**

A Christmas Message

Mr Hawke, thanks for coming in.
It's a great pleasure. Where am I supposed to do this? Is it this camera here? I'm just about organised here.

Probably here. What are you going to say?
I'm going to make a statement to the nation.

What are you going to say?
I'm just going to give my annual message, assessing the position as I see it, offering some message of hope, it being that time of year.

How are you going to offer a message of hope?
I'm not interested in getting into an interview situation with you, I simply want to…

No, no, no, I just wondered what you're going to say.
Well, I'm going to say that this is a time of year when I think Australians are coming together as a nation all over the country.

I wouldn't mention the country.
Don't mention the country. Why not?

Well, people are walking off their farms, regional industries closing down all over the place. It's a bit bleak in the country.
Well, coming together all over the cities then.

I'd keep off the cities if you possibly can.

Why keep off the cities?

Businesses are going over like a house of cards, people are sleeping under bridges in the cities. A couple of the state capitals are actually bankrupt.

Look, I don't want to get into an interview situation with you, I simply want to wish everybody the very best.

Who?

Well look, it's a family occasion, I thought I might start with the family.

Might be a bit patronising, mightn't it? You've had them in a monetarist headlock for eight years, increased the cost of an education, eliminated the prospect of a job and now you want to wish them all a merry whatever.

I don't have to address the family then, I can address a section of the public. The elderly.

OK, that's fine, but stay off super and savings by the way.

Yes, I'd better not mention anybody who's got a house either.

I wouldn't.

Or an income.

No.

Perhaps I won't start with the elderly. I'll address the young, that's what I'll do.

Yes, they'd like to hear from you.

What do you mean?

Well, they've got nothing else to do. Unemployment among the young is thirty per cent. Caring for them is a growth industry.

Is there any particular area especially badly affected?

Australia.

(thoughtfully) Yes, that's true.

Why don't you talk about the Opposition?

Why would anyone talk about the Opposition?

Well it's a time of the year when we put away our differences. John Hewson is a human being after all.

Yes, except he's just announced a plan to change Australia into the type of society we don't want to live in. He's going to reduce the cost of the labour pool by twenty per cent, tax everyone twice and give the money to anyone with a Habsburg chin. You can't take money off the poor and give it to the rich like that and expect to be congratulated at this time of the year.

Aren't the rich the best people to make investment decisions?

They made some bloody stupid investment decisions during the nineteen-eighties, didn't they?

Mr Hawke, who let them do that?

I said I didn't want to get into an interview situation.

I'm just trying to find out what you're going to say, Mr Hawke.

I'm trying to wish everybody a merry Christmas.

Well, it's not going to be all that merry, is it? I wouldn't mention mass either.

Why not?

Because there are people out there who are Muslims, other religions; you're going to offend people.

That's going to give offence? All right, no mass.

And no merry.

No merry?

No merry, no mass.

Am I allowed the rest?

Yes, sure. Go ahead.

My fellow Australians—Christ!

A PRIMATE OF THE CHURCH

On the Ordination of Women

Thanks for joining us.
It's a pleasure.

I wonder if I could ask you, as Primate of the church, about your opposition to the ordination of women...
Could I just pause there momentarily? You say, 'as the Primate of the church'...was that the expression you used?

I thought you were the Primate of the church.
No, I'm *a* primate in the church but I'm certainly not *the* Primate.

How many primates are there?
In the church?

Yes.
There are many thousands of them obviously. Some of them are opposed to the ordination of women and then there's a completely different group of course, who are dead against it.

Are you opposed to the ordination of women?
Yes I am, and could I preempt your next question by saying that this is not a discriminatory thing against, ahm...

Women.

Pardon?

Women.

Where?

No, the discrimination, it's not against women.

Oh no, there's nothing they can do about it. How can they help it? It's just bad luck.

Why are the primates you hang around with opposed to the ordination of women? Aren't some of the primates in favour of the ordination of women?

Yes, some of them are, but most of the ones I hang about with are opposed to it.

Why?

Because it's unconstitutional. The constitution of the church specifically forbids it.

But surely the constitution can be changed?

Under certain circumstances that's possible.

How?

Well, the expression for instance, 'as we move forward into the twelfth century', that was changed.

To 'the twentieth.'

Well, that's a fairly radical suggestion, but we'd certainly give you a hearing.

The point I'm trying to make here is, aren't you cutting the church off from society at the very time when it needs to become relevant to the community?

I beg your pardon. The church is going through a very successful phase just at the moment.

Aren't numbers down?

Numbers are not down, no. I was at the church this afternoon and the turnout was extremely encouraging.

What was the occasion?
The occasion will interest you actually. It was the birthday of one of our very youngest members in the congregation; young Terry.

How old was he?
Young Terry?

Yes.
He'd be 87.

Look, can I ask where you're going to get people entering the ministry if you're not going to allow women who are otherwise fully qualified to get in?
Obviously we're going to recruit from the ranks of men.

But where are they going to come from?
There are plenty of people. I, for instance, could have a try.

You could be ordained as a minister?
Of course.

But what are your qualifications?
(*rising from seat, his hands going towards his fly*) I'll show you my qualifications. (*freeze*)

**MR R J HAWKE,
RECENTLY RETIRED PRIME MINISTER**

Responding to Suggestions that His Resignation Lacked Dignity

Mr Hawke, thanks for joining us.
It's a very great pleasure and it's nice to be back.

There's been some criticism this week of the way you went about your resignation.
I wouldn't worry too much about criticism, I'm pretty inured to criticism. As a matter of fact there was some criticism in the period immediately prior to my resigning.

For how long?
Nearly nine years.

But on the matter of your resignation, how do you respond to people who say you shouldn't…
Look, I've just about had it with this drivel about how I am and am not to conduct my…I don't need the morals committee, frankly. I've got a perfect right to conduct myself commercially as I will; I wanted a life after politics, I made that plain.

...no, no, what I meant was...

If I hadn't chosen to serve this country in such a lengthy, a famously, ennoblingly fabulous period as Prime Minister...

...Mr Hawke...

Could I just point out that this answer is being brought to you by Delmonte suits? That extra notch of elegance, that extra touch of class in a Delmonte suit?

Mr Hawke, you do realise how the public have reacted to this resignation?

(his suit gone, now in a red T-shirt with 'Coke' in large letters) Well obviously it's very tragic. They feel this, clearly. It's a great loss. A great loss for the entire Labor Party.

What's been lost?

Well, Wills probably, the way things are going at the moment. Do you want a break?

I'm sorry?

(holding up chocolate bar) Do you want a KitKat break?

My Hawke, don't you think they have a point though?

The public? Aren't they happy?

No they're not.

(to camera) Perhaps they should try Rectanol.

Mr Hawke, if I could just change the subject for a second, how do you think the Government's doing?

(now in baseball cap, clutching mineral water bottle in one hand, and a large bottle of PepsiCola under his other arm) I think the government's doing very well. *(in advertising voice)* Better ideas, sooner; with a Labor Government.

What are they going to do?

Well, they're going to fix the economy; they're going to inject about two billion dollars into it in order to kickstart the upturn.

Is Mr Keating a Keynesian now?

(*now with packet of VitaBrits and different mineral water*) A Keynesian? No, I think he's a Leo, but you seem to have missed the point.

Well what is the point?

The point is they've now got the economy to the point where they can fix it.

(*in front of interviewer, prominently, is Hawke's foot in an Adidas shoe*) **Is the package ready?**

(*still with Adidas-clad foot outstretched at camera*) Well, I'm not intimately aware of the day-to-day running of government, but my impression is it's nearly finished, it's almost there.

What have they got to do?

They've just got to change a little bit of wording here and there.

What sort of thing?

(*now with Akubra, KitKat lodged in hatband*) Well, they can't very well call it Mayday Mayday, which is what it's known as around the office; there's an entire section of it called Gawdhelpus If This Doesn't Work, they could probably do better than that. Cata-Strophe, there's another section called Cata-Strophe.

Catastrophe.

What?

Catastrophe.

That's not a bad idea, how do you spell that? Just write it down will you?

Mr Hawke, thanks very much. And I take it you're enjoying your retirement?

(*voiceover, singing: 'Oh what a feeling!' Hawke does Toyota leap and freezes in mid-air*)

**MR R J HAWKE,
'60 MINUTES' INTERVIEWER**

A Reversal of Roles

Bob Hawke, in his new career as a television interviewer, is in the unaccustomed position of interrogating the man who usually asks the questions.

Thank you very much for coming in.

It's a pleasure.
How have you been? Good?

I've been terrific, thanks.
Have a good break?

Great break, thanks. How've you been?
How do I look? Do I look good?

You look great.
Do I look fantastic?

Yes, you look great.
Obviously there are a lot of things I'd like to ask you about. Clearly, over recent years, the focus in this country has been on me because I've been Prime Minister for such a famously long and successful period of time.

Sure.
Having the most important job, the number one job…

Sure.

...in the country, being the most important person in the country...*(to producer)* Don't cut to him! No, no, don't cut to him! I realise the interview is with him, but don't cut to him. I haven't even asked him a question yet.

I'm sorry.

Eh?

I'm sorry.

No, no it's not your fault. *(to producer)* Don't cut to him. I haven't asked him the question. *(to interviewer)* Obviously the focus has been on me because of my enormous prominence...

Sure.

...and I think that's natural. But we want to talk about you now.

Sure, OK.

What did you think of me when I was Prime Minister? Wasn't it fabulous? Wasn't that a brilliant period? Wasn't that a spectacular, scintillating period in recent Australian political history?

Well, I...

Wasn't that fantastic? I bet you remember where you were on the night in 1983 when I got into office. Where were you on that night, just talking about you for a moment?

I was in Adelaide.

Wasn't I brilliant? Wasn't I absolutely brilliant? You remember that? Etched on the nation's memory I think, that night.

Yes, yes, I...

Are you going to cry?

I'm sorry?

Aren't you going to cry at some point in the interview? It would help the interview a great deal. It would be bigger than Texas if you cried at some point.

I don't know if I can cry to order.

Can't you just think of something that upsets you? That's what I always used to do. Just fix on something you know is going to reduce you to absolutely racking sobs. I can help. I can ask about it. Just think about something that makes you break down and cry uncontrollably.

Ask me about Australia.

About Australia?

Yes.

Who do you reckon is the greatest Prime Minister Australia's ever seen?

Ahmm…

(helping) Hoh…hoh…starts with hoh…

Peter Hollingworth?

No, Haw… Haw…

Fred Hollows.

Cut!

I'm sorry…

Man's a bloody idiot. Will you get me someone I can interview please?

(interviewer dissolves into tears)

**SENATOR KIM BEAZLEY,
MINISTER FOR EDUCATION**

The Clever Country

Mr Beazley, thanks for your time.

It's a great pleasure, always happy to talk about the Clever Country campaign, which we'll be advancing in ensuing months, thanks for inviting me in.

I actually wanted to talk to you about this police video that surfaced this week, featuring the white Australians dressed as Aborigines. You must have been appalled by this.

You're talking about a *police* video? I'm the Minister for Education. You are aware of that?

What are we going do about it?

I'm not sure that it falls precisely within the ambit of the Minister for Education.

Don't you think we've got to change our attitudes on these questions, as a community?

Well clearly. We can't have this sort of nineteenth-century attitude permeating our own race relations. But on the other hand Australia's got a very good record in representing the views of oppressed minorities.

Overseas.

I believe that's where it happens, yes.

But how are we going to change our own attitudes?
I am the Minister for Education, sunshine. I'm not sure that I'm the boy to ask!

Well, guess.
Oh, a big advertising campaign, plenty of booming music, lots of drums, anthem-quality, idiots jumping about the place, black people, white people, that sort of thing.

Like the Bicentennial.
Yes, only a campaign that makes sense, with any luck.

How can you change society's attitudes without education?
Look, frankly in education we're pretty flat stick maintaining literacy and imparting a few basic facts about counting. I'm not sure we can deal with the alteration of a national consciousness.

My point is, racism does seem to be a fundamental human characteristic though, doesn't it?
Perhaps it is.

Well, doesn't every generation need to be educated out of it?
We do study Australian history, I think a lot of people are very well aware of our growth as a nation.

Since Cook.
Since Cook by all means, but before Cook as well.

What happened before that?
Before Cook got here?

Yes.
He was getting ready to leave, as I understand it; popping a few things on the boat, and getting one of those things you locate the sun with.

I'm talking about before that. What about 40,000 years ago?
We study that too, Ancient Egypt, Rome, European architecture, Etruscan pottery...

Mr Beazley, let me take another line: what examples do we learn of oppression and genocide?
Plenty of that; we study Spain in South America, Belgium in the Congo, Japan in Asia…

The police in Australia.
Yes, you can study that if you want.

Where do you study that?
In a court. If you want to study that I'd get down there now.

Mr Beazley, thanks for joining us.
Don't you want to ask me about the Clever Country?

No, I just wanted to ask you a couple of questions about Australia.

**A NEWSPAPER EDITOR,
46, OF SYDNEY**

A Matter of Principle

Thanks for coming in.
It's a pleasure to be here, thank you.

Can I ask you, as editor of one of the major daily newspapers, do you support the idea of Australia's becoming a republic?
Yes we do, but I should point out that we're not the only player in the market obviously, and I can only speak for our organisation. We don't have the whole market.

How much of it do you have?
At the moment?

Yes.
Ninety-three per cent at the moment, but we're talking to the Government. We think it's a bit restrictive.

So as a newspaper do you support the republican push?
Yes, we do by and large. We think it's time Australia grew up. We're not English. We're Australian. Different hemisphere, different country, different history, completely different pattern of post-war migration. We think it's time we matured, and walked into the sunlit upland of our own destiny. Incidentally, did you know that Fergie and Randy Andy have given it away?

Do you think the republican issue will figure in the federal election?

Yes, we do, we think it's probably one of the main issues that's going to dominate in the next couple of months, here's a photo of Fergie with a bloke from America. *(handing photo to interviewer)* The old Andy was away on manoeuvres if you know what I mean, nudge kick wink say no more. Here's another one. This is a beauty—you tell me what that is. *(handing him another photo)* That is Princess Di's knee. That's taken from the back. Nude.

Princess Di's knee?

Now, can you tell me where Charlie Boy is in that photo? Can you see a bloke who looks like the FA Cup? He's not there is he?

He's not there; what does this mean?

Could be all over for another royal marriage, couldn't it? Of course the person I bleed for is the Queen.

So you're swinging right behind the movement to make Australia a republic?

Absolutely. We're rock solid behind the republican movement, don't worry about that.

Is it in tomorrow's paper?

High, wide and handsome in tomorrow's paper, yes.

Have you got a headline?

Huge headline; huge headline.

What is it?

Get Off Our Backs Pommy Mongrels. Queen's Dog Farts At Races.

Anything about racism?

Racism is all finished, isn't it? Went out of existence.

Not there any more?

Didn't they vote it out of existence on Wednesday night?

In South Africa yes, but what about here?

Well it wouldn't happen here. I'd have noticed it in the paper. I run it.

Yeah, sure. Thanks for joining us.
Have you heard about Prince Edward?

No.
You know he's a teapot?

A what?
I'm a republican myself, of course.

**MR PETER WALSH,
EX-SENATOR AND FINANCE MINISTER**

The View from Outside the Compound

Mr Walsh, thanks for coming in.
Mmm?

Thanks for your time.
Oh, it'd be about five to seven I should think.

You've been critical of the One Nation package, haven't you?
I have been critical of the package, yes. However, I wouldn't have thought I was completely alone in that.

What are your criticisms of it?
Well, I've made a well-reasoned argument. I would suggest if you're interested in what I think, you read what I had to say.

I have read it.
Well how come you don't know what I think about it?

Well, a lot of people aren't sure of what you're saying in all this.
Look, are you interested in this because of your breathtaking ability to get your little brain across macroeconomic issues, or do you simply want to stir up as much trouble as possible for the Government?

Mr Walsh, I'm interested in the economic package, obviously.
Well there's not much point in talking to me then.

Why not?
Because I'm just interested in making as much trouble for the Government as I possibly can.

But you were a *member* of the Government.
Yes, that was a bit limiting, but I've put a couple of laps on the field since I got out, I'll tell you that for nothing.

Why did you get out?
Good behaviour.

No, what I mean is wouldn't you have been better placed to improve economic policy if you'd stayed on as an economic minister?
It's a bit hard to dump on economic policy with any real weight if you're running one of the economic ministries.

Why do you want to dump on economic policy? Isn't that the job of the Opposition?
It would be the job of the Opposition if they showed the slightest inclination to do it but they don't.

So you're helping them.
Helping the Opposition?

Yes.
I beg your humble pardon, I wouldn't give them the time of day. I'm helping the Government.

How?
By keeping the Opposition out of the papers.

Yes but you're doing it by criticising Government policy.
Well, someone's got to. The country's lost its way.

Oh come on, Mr Walsh...

The Governor-General got thrown out of his local RSL the other night because of his republican leanings. I think we're out of radio range aren't we?

Mr Walsh, are you just saying all this to make a name for yourself or do you actually believe it yourself?

Yes.

Which?

Don't you call me a witch, old boy, or I'll clout you right off that chair and into that wall.

Mr Walsh, what have you been doing since you left Parliament?

Oh, just running the charm school. And a little paper-folding. I make these rather beautiful, delicate birds out of folded paper. I fold the paper in such a way as to render a rather exquisite bird.

And what do you do with them?

When I've finished them?

Yes.

I sit on them.

Mr Walsh, thanks for your time.

Shut up.

DR TERRY METHERELL, EX-MINISTER IN THE NSW GREINER GOVERNMENT. RESIGNED FROM MINISTRY BUT RETAINED SEAT ON PROMISE OF EXECUTIVE POSITION WITH ENVIRONMENT PROTECTION AUTHORITY.

The Selection Process

Dr Metherell, thanks for coming in.
(via satellite from Vanuatu; in floral holiday shirt, potted palm in the background) Oh, that's a very great pleasure, thank you.

Where are you at the moment?
I'll just ask, hang on a minute. *(to someone out of camera)* What's the name of the area we're in at the moment? Really? *(to interviewer)* We're in the region of about a hundred and ten thousand.

No, I mean geographically.
You know where a hundred thousand is?

Yes.
Ten degrees north.

Are you in the capital?
Oh yes, rolling in it. We should be all right for a bit now.

You've been appointed to a position at the Environment Protection Authority.
Yes I have. Haven't you?

No.

Really? I thought if I'd got one they must be coming out in cereal packets.

It's quite an important job.
Oh yes, it's a terribly important job. It's with the... *(he can't remember)*

Environment Protection Authority?
Yes, it's with them. It's a very important area, the whole area of the, um... *(he can't remember)*

Environment?
Hmm?

Environment?
Yes, high priority for the um... *(he can't remember)*

Greiner Government.
Yes, I heard that, I think that's probably why he made the appointment personally.

But Dr Metherell, you left the Greiner Government.
Yes, of course I did. One of the most reprehensible governments I've ever seen, probably anywhere on earth.

In that case why did he appoint you to this position?
Well, he's protecting his environment, isn't he?

Yes, but why did you accept it?
I'm protecting mine too, that's the nature of the job, it's an environment protection job.

Can I ask you, what are your qualifications for the position?
About a hundred and ten thousand. *(to someone off camera)* Will you get me one of those drinks with an umbrella in it?

Why wasn't the job advertised?
It was advertised. I have seen comment that it wasn't advertised, but that is a calculated lie. It was advertised.

Whereabouts?

On the back of the cheque.

What did it say?

It said a hundred and ten thousand.

No, on the back Dr Metherell, what did it say?

Oh, I've got it here—'Happy birthday to you, Happy birthday to you. Good job going at EPA. Applicant must be Terry Metherell'.

Do you think people are cynical about politicians?

Oh, I shouldn't think so.

Why not?

It's a democracy, they run it.

Who runs it?

The people run a democracy, that's what the word means, look it up some time. *Demo*, meaning people, *cracy* ...

Meaning?

Pardon?

What does *cracy* mean?

About a hundred and ten thousand.

**THE HON. NICK GREINER,
PREMIER OF NEW SOUTH WALES**

Safeguards for the Public

Mr Greiner, thanks for coming in.
Thank you, it's a pleasure.

You seem to be in a bit of strife over this job you've given to Terry Metherell.
Look, I wonder if I could make one thing quite clear.

Certainly.
If it's not too much trouble.

Certainly.
If I'm not bothering you too much by clarifying something.

No, of course.
Thank you very much, that's good.

What is it?
What's what?

What's the thing you want to make clear?
I haven't got anything at the moment, but should anything clarify itself in my mind I'd like to know I have the opportunity to express it.

Why did you give a mate a job?
Metherell is not a mate of mine, Metherell's never been a mate of mine ...

Oh come on Mr Greiner...
In fact, Metherell's one of the biggest pr..., ahmm...

Problems?
Bit of a problem for the Government, the old Metherell.

So why did you give him this job?
I didn't give him a job...

Mr Greiner, you gave him a job...
Dr Metherell applied for, and got, on merit, a position with the EPA.

He's well qualified for the position?
He's very well qualified for the position.

What are his qualifications?
Let me rephrase that: he's spectacularly *un*qualified for any other position I've ever given him.

But you are now under pressure to withdraw the offer of that job, aren't you?
Yes, of course I am. There'll always be people who disagree with an appointment of this type.

And who are they?
Look them up in the phone book. There are plenty of people whose name isn't Greiner.

So what are you going to do?
I'm going to introduce legislation ensuring that this sort of thing doesn't happen again.

How do you do that?
Well, you introduce new laws preventing me, I mean preventing the Prime Minister...

Premier.

What?

Premier.

...the Premier, should he be unscrupulous and cynical of course, from using his power, by parking someone who is either a very good friend or in this case a complete pr...

Problem.

Bit of a problem, in a safe job where they can be kept out of the way.

And Terry Metherell wasn't even a mate.

No. Complete waste of a job.

So, do you think the calibre of person who goes into politics these days is a cause of concern in the community?

Yes I do, and I agree with the community, if Terry Metherell hadn't gone into politics it wouldn't have been necessary for me, that is, for the Premier, to behave in a way that obliges me—the Premier—to bring about a change in the law to prevent it from happening again.

So you think this will settle the matter?

It had better, unless I—unless the Premier—brings in some new legislation to prevent me—to prevent the Premier—from doing a deal with the independents because my power base—his power base—is so debilitated that if I'm not, if he's not, if they're not, if the Premiers aren't careful, they might have to do something like go to the people.

Yeah. Mr Greiner, thank you both for coming in.

Oh, thank you. Half of us are delighted.

**SENATOR GRAHAM RICHARDSON,
MINISTER FOR ALL SORTS OF THINGS
AND FAMILY MAN**

A Storm Brewing

Senator Richardson, thanks for coming in.
It's a very great pleasure.

You were accused of impropriety this week.
Yes I was, but only by the Opposition.

Yes, but you were accused of not having declared an interest in a radio station while you were helping to formulate broadcasting policy.
Yes, a minor matter, I simply overlooked the fact when I declared.

Were you asked?
Yes, you're obliged to declare any interests when you go into government.

And you forgot to declare a directorship in a radio station?
Yes, a minor oversight though. I was very, very, *very* busy at the time.

What were you doing?
I was helping to formulate broadcasting policy, I think.

What *did* you declare?
Under interests?

Yes.
'Gardening', I think I put.

You were also accused of trying to influence the Government of the Marshall Islands over a case involving an Australian who'd been charged with forgery.

Well yes, but mind you, I know something about that case.

What did you do?

I simply rang up a government official in the relevant atoll to see what was going on.

Who was the official?

I think he might have been the Prime Minister from memory, but I certainly didn't exert any undue influence.

What did you say?

I said 'This is Graham Richardson here, obviously ringing as a private individual, you may have heard of me, I'm a senior government minister with your biggest trading partner, I wonder if I could make an inquiry about my cousin's extremely innocent husband.'

Did the Foreign Minister know you were making the call?

Yes, I spoke to Gareth Evans prior to making the call, obviously.

What did you say?

I asked him if he enjoyed being Foreign Minister, I mentioned a couple of other positions that were going if he got a bit sick of it.

What sort of positions?

Well, the toilets are filthy in some of the branch offices, I just thought I may be able to hook him an alternative job.

On another note, I take it you were happy with the CPI result.

Total vindication of government policy. Zero CPI. We can splash a bit of money about now.

What are you planning to do?

Well, obviously we're going to celebrate the end of the recession. Our economic troubles are over, we're going to spend some money.

How are you going to do it?

Well, we're going to provide every single Australian with a helicopter.

With a helicopter?

Yes. Each. One helicopter per person. Every Australian citizen will be provided with a helicopter.

What will they do with a helicopter?

Well, if they hear of a job vacancy going on the other side of town, they'll be able to get there a lot faster.

This sounds pretty expensive. What happens if you haven't got the money?

We may have to marry a government minister into a branch of the Bond family but we'll stop at nothing, let me tell you.

Finally, what do you say to the unemployed in Australia at the moment?

Well look, obviously we're talking to the unemployed constantly at the moment.

About what?

About the flag, mainly.

A MAFIA SPOKESPERSON

On Gang Warfare

Thanks for coming in.
(in Godfather drawl) Oh it's a pleasure you know, don't worry about it.

You're back in Australia.
No, we're not backin' Australia, I don't know why anyone would back Australia, you know. I'm greatly opposed to what's going on here.

Why?
You can't do no business here, you've got a syndicate here's got the whole country wrapped up. I can't make no headway, know what I mean?

What's this syndicate?
We don't know who they are. They're working out of Sydney.

Oh, the New South Wales Right.
I don't know their names, I met them in a carpark, it was night-time, I don't know…

Was it Mr Keating?
Keating? Dark guy? With the suit? And the shoes? Maybe looks like one of the Righteous Brothers?

Yes, that's him.

Yes, there was another guy too, a guy they call Richo.

Graham Richardson.

With the tall hair?

Yes.

Maybe looks like a bouncer?

Yes.

Maybe for a cake shop?

Yes, that's him. Does he have a bandage on his foot?

Yeah, he does now, yes.

He has gout.

Yes, we give him the gout the other night, in the carpark.

You gave him the gout?

Yes, we give him the gout again if he don't clean up his goddamn act. We maybe give him the gout a little higher, you know, and in the middle.

How did you give him the gout?

Well, you know, we accidentally pop a slug into his foot maybe when we're having a little word with him about the family.

Aren't you the family?

Yeah, but I tell you, if our family was going as well as Richo's family we ain't got no goddamn problem, you know what I mean?

What does Richo's family do?

Maybe they in business, you know. Maybe in the immigration area, you want a little passport, maybe you go see someone, I don't know.

Isn't there a problem with this at the moment?

Yeah, there is. That's why we give Richo the gout, in the foot, with the shooter, you know what I mean.

Right—so he'd make up his mind.
Make his mind up, you know.

What do you think he'll do?
If he don't want the gout?

Yes.
Maybe he should retire, maybe grow some nice roses. Maybe take the dog for a walk, you know what I mean?

Yes, sure. Have you spoken to the Opposition?
Yeah, the feeble-minded dude with the red car?

Yes.
Yes, no problem. We ain't got no problem with the feeble-minded dude.

Why's that?
Well, I tell him about the gout. He don't want the gout. 'No gout,' he says, 'spare me the goddamn gout.' This Richo, though, we gotta fix him.

Sure. Thanks again for joining us.
You better be grateful.

**DR TERRY METHERELL,
EX-MINISTER IN THE NSW GREINER
GOVERNMENT**

Dear Laws of Evidence

Dr Metherell, thanks for joining us.
Pleasure.

You've stirred up a fair old mess this week.
Well, I stirred it up a while ago, I've just been reading it out this week.

This is from your diary?
My excellent, meticulous and very well-kept diary, yes.

Dr Metherell, how is it possible for you to give evidence before a Corruption Commission, in which you contend it is corrupt for the Premier to have proposed a deal with you, while on the other hand it's not corrupt for you to have accepted it?
That's a very astute question to which there is a very astute answer, and that is that I had no idea that there was any possibility the deal might be construed as corrupt at the time it was proposed to me.

Then what did you think?
I can tell you what I thought, it's in my diary, I can quote it directly to you *(reads)*: 'Nick just proposed a deal to me. It doesn't sound corrupt to me. The weather continues beautiful.'

So you were being offered a $150,000 a year job with a guarantee they'd find you something else if it fell through?
Yes, and I'd resign from the Parliament.

A pretty standard agreement.
Pretty standard, and I'd be working in an area which interested me a great deal.

With an organisation whose director opposed the appointment.
Yes, very challenging job indeed.

And so obvious were your qualifications for this position that your appointment was kept secret?
Well, only until the Governor was informed.

Why was that?
Well obviously the Governor has to formally approve any such appointments in a democ…, a deming…, a demongratule…,

Democracy?
Who?

Democracy.
Whatever, yeah.

So, when did you find out about this appointment?
Well, I can tell you exactly when I did, it was on the fifteenth according to this. I'll read it to you: 'This will serve to introduce my cousin's husband Greg Sy…' Oh, hang on, somebody's been using this to press on. Here it is: 'Got up, had a call from Brad, had a meeting in a carpark with Nick. Stood on one leg up a tree in Dee Why singing the Ave Maria, had lunch with Brad, met Biggles and Ginger round the back of the ops room, wrote *Hamlet*, ran into Beethoven in a milkbar, thrashed him 6-1, 6-0, 6-0, invented a round thing that runs along the ground, went home, went to bed and had a dream about a Viennese doctor.'

What do think Mr Greiner will do?
Oh, five years I should think.

Why do you say that?
It's a five-year diary. That's why I bought it—it's a five-year diary.

(looking over Metherell's shoulder) **Dr Metherell, there's a man in a white coat here looking for you.**
Oh, that'll be my driver; *(calling over his shoulder)* I'll be with you in a minute Dr Driver! Are we just about finished?

I think you are.
(calling again to 'driver', pointing back to interviewer) He agrees!

**MR ALAN BOND,
RETIRED YACHTSMAN**

An Investment Opportunity

Mr Bond, thanks for coming in.
I'm not in yet. The matter is still proceeding. I'm still out at the moment.

But you're appealing.
That's very kind of you. Thanks very much.

I mean, your lawyers are appealing.
A lot of people don't think so but I think they're pretty good. I think they're doing a very good job.

You didn't have much of a week this week did you?
Couldn't take a trick earlier, but things perked up a bit today.

You're not on the list of Australia's ten richest people any more.
No, I'm not, but you'll note that two of my sons are.

Really? What do they do?
Do? They don't do anything, they're among the richest people in the country.

But where did they get the money?
Well, it's old money.

What old money?

Any old money, frankly, that we could still find lying about.

So what are you doing now?

I've got plenty on. I've got a very exciting new development in Western Australia. Lovely new units that were just finalised today. I can fit you in there, if you're interested in investing in units.

What is it?

It's in South Perth, beautifully positioned, all self-contained, exquisite, government-backed.

How many bedrooms?

One bedroom, but it's got the lot, everything's in there and there's a sort of a communal area where all of the facilities are housed. It's a totally new concept in urban dwelling.

So it's like a retirement village type of idea?

It's very like a retirement village type of idea, yes, for business people in Australia who are a bit jaded after a lifetime of service to the community.

Like yourself.

Yes.

And is it quiet?

Oh, very quiet, yes. Someone could scream to death in the next room and you wouldn't hear a sausage.

What about a view?

Yes, beautiful views. Panoramic views.

So the units are elevated?

No, the windows are elevated.

Security?

Oh, groaning with security. You can't get in, the walls are this thick and there's a guard on the gate. Very secure.

And are they expensive?
I could do you one for about two hundred and eighty, two seventy-five, best price two sixty.

Mmm. Is there any interest from overseas or is it a local project?
Yes, there is interest overseas, we've got somebody from Spain coming into one of the units, probably later this year. Into the Penthouse unit.

Oh, so there's an upper level.
No actually, there isn't, but he didn't know that when he bought it.

But you expect them to sell pretty well.
I expect them to be chocka by Christmas at the present rate.

And so anyone interested should get in touch with you?
Yes. Contact my office. Speak to Mr G. Overnor, he's managing the property for us.

Mr Overnor.
Yes, or Mr D. Eputygovernor if he's busy.

Is there a deposit?
There is in some of the units, yes, but we'll clean them out pretty severely before you come in.

And so you're still very busy.
I've got plenty of ideas, I've got a swag of stuff to get through.

Like what?
I've got to redirect the mail, get a toothbrush, talk to the milkman—I've got a list here somewhere—cancel the papers. I've got plenty of things to do.

Well Alan Bond, see you again.
Eh?

See you again.
How soon do you reckon?

**THE HON. BARRY JONES,
CHAIRMAN OF THE AUSTRALIAN
LABOR PARTY**

Parent-Teacher Night

Mr Jones, thanks for coming in.
Thank you very much, and good evening.

And congratulations on your appointment this week.
Thank you very much, difficult job, great challenge.

You're lucky to have a job.
That's true, good thing I'm not young, I wouldn't have stood a chance.

It's not going to be easy taking over in the middle of the year is it?
No, it isn't and of course they've got some very serious tests coming up; we'll need to get on with it.

So you'll be keeping the work up to them will you?
Yes I will, and I think they need a much more structured programme.

Will this involve more homework?
Probably a great deal more homework, yes; was there anyone in particular here you were interested in?

Paul—Paul Keating.
Paul Keating. Well Paul as you know is a bright enough lad and greatly enjoying being head boy, after being deputy head for so long.

But is he getting any work done? We don't see any evidence of anything significant that he's doing.

Well, he's certainly been putting in the hours. Did you see the project he did on cable television for instance?

Yes, we did.

Did a great deal of work but he didn't answer the question. I mean, he needs to organise himself. Did you have a chance to talk to him about that project?

Well we tried, but he kept changing his mind all the time about what he thought.

I don't think he thought *anything*, did he? There was no evidence of it.

He seems to be a member of some sort of gang.

Well, boys of that age, you know what they're like; some of these boys are perfectly all right, some of them are a bit of a problem.

What about this young Richardson?

Graham Richardson? A typical example, and he may have to repeat a year I think.

John Dawkins?

Paul and John have been helping each other with their maths, haven't they?

Yes, but they both got an F.

That's true, they didn't exactly bolt in, did they?

Well, is there anything we can do at home?

Does Paul read a lot? He doesn't strike me as being a well-informed boy.

Well, we hardly ever see him. He's never home.

Well perhaps you should take him out, introduce him to some kids, some unemployed kids. I'm sure they'd love to talk to somebody like Paul.

I don't think so; he hides in his bedroom and he won't come out.

Well look, we'll do what we can; obviously we'll be giving him extra maths, extra English.

Extra history.

Extra history, by all means.

Economics?

I don't think Paul's doing economics is he? No, he's not down here as having anything to do with economics.

Yes, yes he is. He told us he was doing economics today.

No. Double sport, lunch, and a school visit to a piggery this afternoon.

But he told us he was coming top in it.

As far as I know he's not doing economics at all.

We thought he was coming in dux.

Oh, we don't pry into their private lives. I mean the school can't do everything.

THE HON. JOHN DAWKINS, TREASURER

The Great Communicator

Mr Dawkins, thanks for joining us.
Thank you, it's a pleasure to be here.

I wonder if I could ask you about the economic recovery.
By all means, what would you like to know about it?

In what century do you think it'll happen?
Well, I think we're already beginning to get certain initial indications that the start of what we hope might be an economic recovery...

Mr Dawkins...
...is beginning to manifest itself in certain pockets of the economic model...

Mr Dawkins...
...I think the situation's really quite hopeful.

Mr Dawkins, how do you think the recovery will be affected by the next ice-age?
The problem you see is that we're in the grip of a global recession and I think people appreciate that...

Mr Dawkins...hullo, hullo?

...and I think that the microeconomic reform program we've embarked on is going to strengthen the fundamental model...

Mr Dawkins? It doesn't matter what I ask you, does it?

So that when the economic recovery does begin to bite we'll be in a much stronger overall position.

Mr Dawkins, did you get to the football the other night?

We've got short-term interest rates pegged to around six point five per cent, which of course means...

Mr Dawkins, wave if you can hear me.

...which of course means that when recovery does begin to bite it will be sustainable in terms of low inflation.

Mr Dawkins, you keep saying the same thing all the time.

I don't keep saying the same thing.

You keep saying the same thing.

I don't keep saying the same thing.

You keep saying the same thing.

I *don't* keep saying the same thing.

Mr Dawkins...

I do not keep saying the same thing.

...you keep saying the same thing.

I don't keep saying the same thing, certainly not all the time.

Mr Dawkins, what about the people? What are you supposed to do in this country if you're not a major financial institution?

Well look, I'm running Treasury; we operate on a pretty big scale up there, I don't quite know what you're talking about.

You keep saying the same thing. I'm talking about things like youth unemployed.

There are no youth unemployed.

Mr Dawkins...
There are, by all means, rather a lot of non-elderly transitional units in the Australian employment market but youth unemployment in Australia is among the lowest in the OECD.

How low?
Four.

Four per cent?
No, four people.

Four young people out of work?
Four or five. It may have crept up as high as five.

What about education, social welfare, small business, health?
Well, hang on, you've mentioned three or four other portfolios there. Why don't you speak to these other ministers?

Mr Dawkins, you know that it's all indexed to the economy. What are *you* going to do?
What are *you* going to do about it, are you just going to sit there and complain? What are people doing in this country? Do they expect me to fix everything?

What are they supposed to do?
Why don't you get a grant and turn this into a movie?

How would I do that?
Apply. Do you know anyone in Treasury?

No.
Oh well, you haven't got a chance. There's your problem.

Mr Dawkins, thanks for joining us.
Mmm?

Mr Dawkins, thanks for joining us.
Don't you know *anyone* in Treasury?

Well, I know you.
Yes, but I just keep saying the same thing.

**THE HON. PAUL KEATING,
PRIME MINISTER**

Women on Stamps

Mr Keating, thanks for your time.
It's a pleasure, thank you.

I wonder if I could ask you about the Australian economy.
Oh not the economy again, every time you ask me...I reckon you're obsessed, you people. Why don't you get your minds up above your trousers? Ask me about something else.

Mr Keating, you've been running the economy now for ten years. You keep saying it's in recovery and we keep getting figures that say it isn't.
Oh, I think I'm probably a little more experienced at reading the figures than you are, aren't I?

Mr Keating, we've got the highest unemployment in sixty years.
I thought you wanted to talk about the economy.

I do.
You're talking about unemployment. The economy's fine. Why don't you ask me about something that matters?

What matters more than the economy?
Oh, for heaven's sake, the most important question in this country is how we're going to get some women on the stamps.

Women on stamps?

Yes. What sort of society do we want to live in here?

A solvent one.

You want to wait until I've finished?

Yes.

Thank you. We've got to fight the idea that you can't put women on stamps.

Mr Keating, there are plenty of women on stamps.

Not enough women on not enough stamps, in my opinion. I'm going to put a lot of women on stamps.

Mr Keating, how will it help the economy if you increase the number of women on stamps?

Oh dear me, you're going to have repeat a year, aren't you? Some of the stamps don't have women on them at all; I saw one in Perth the other day with a tree on it!

How many stamps are you thinking of making?

Nine point five million in the first run, different woman on each one. You'll be able to go out and buy the woman of your choice on a stamp.

What would have to happen for you to admit the Australian economy isn't working...

We're going to need some children on stamps as well, as a matter of interest.

...and the Government policy hasn't worked?

Some small-business stamps out by Christmas.

Some farming stamps?

Yes, a very good idea, featuring all those things we used to do in this country.

Aboriginal stamps?

Aboriginal stamps, an excellent idea. You're not the clown you look.

Some stamps with everybody on them except the Government?
Yes, dirty great big stamps, colour and movement, exactly the right sort of thing.

Can they do that sort of thing?
What, put fifteen million heads on the front of a stamp? I should think so, yes.

Where?
Oh, Taiwan, Hong Kong, Korea.

Why can't we do it here?
In Australia?

Yes.
Well, you've got to put glue on the back of them.

We can make glue in this country, surely.
Glue, what out of?

Flour and water.
Oh yes, but you've got to use Malaysian flour and they get the water from France and they stir it up.

With what?
Oh I don't know, some bloke in Japan does it. With a stick, it's like a big matchstick.

Where's it from?
Well, where do we get our matches from?

Finland?
Well we'll get one from Finland then.

So it's Finnish?
Thank God for that.

**THE HON. JOHN HEWSON,
LEADER OF THE LIBERAL PARTY**

Rapping with the Duds

Dr Hewson, thanks for joining us.
Thank you, it's a pleasure to be here.

I wonder if I could talk to you about unemployment.
You're not happy with the work I'm doing here?

Not yours in particular, I meant unemployment in general.
Oh, so you're not talking about a real problem.

Well, it's a real enough problem for the unemployed.
Oh yes, I beg your pardon, oh yes indeed it is, a very real problem, very real, particularly for the young, particularly for the young!

Dr Hewson, you said this week that having spent an hour or so talking to some young unemployed people, you were now aware of their problems.
Yes indeed, I spent an hour or so just shooting the wind with some young unemployed people during the week.

Shooting the breeze.
Yes, I was just knocking the fat around the flag-pole with a few of the funky hepcats.

I'm not sure I completely understand you.

Well, perhaps you're a bit out of date. I was simply, as I say, spending a couple of hours this week just rapping with the duds.

The duds?

Yes, just myself and the duds, just putting a few zephyrs out of their misery…

…Shooting the breeze…

…yes, with some of the funky duds.

With the duds?

Some of the duds. *(looking to someone off camera)* What do you mean it's got an E in it? *(to interviewer)* Hang on a minute. *(looking off)* An E in duds? There's no E in duds, don't be silly… Well where? Duddies? Duddies? Oh, dudes. *(to interviewer)* Hang on a minute, they're not duds, they're dudes.

What did the dudes have to say?

The dudes are very unhappy. There's thirty-five per cent unemployment among the dudes.

What's your solution to all this?

Well, we'll be introducing a completely new policy.

What's it called?

The new policy?

Yes.

Slavery.

Slavery. You're going to introduce slavery.

Well, we won't be calling it slavery, obviously. We've got a new name for it.

What's that?

The new name?

Yes.

For slavery?

Yes.

Freedom.

And how will that work?

There will be a slave wage…

…A freedom wage.

I beg your pardon, yes, a freedom wage.

How much?

Three dollars an hour.

The dole's worth more than that!

They won't be getting the dole. When you become a slave you'll stop being a dud.

A dude.

Oh all right, then, I'll see you later. Bye.

**THE HON. PAUL KEATING,
PRIME MINISTER**

Is There Any Point?

Mr Keating, thanks for joining us.
It's a very great pleasure, thank you.

Thanks for coming in.
It's a very great pleasure, thank you.

Thanks for your time.
It's a very great pleasure, thank you.

Well it's very good of you to find the time.
(slightly exasperated) It's a very great pleasure to find the time to come in and talk to you, thank you very much.

(grinning vacantly) **Thank you very much.**
It's the least I can do, thank *you* very much. Have you got any questions? Got anything you want to ask me?

What about?
About how we're going in this country. About the economic recovery for instance.

Is there any point?
Is there any point? I'm the Prime Minister, old boy. I'm not in a bad position to answer any questions you might have.

Yes, but you don't seem to be responsible for any of the problems.

No we're not, but we're doing what we can to fix them.

What are you doing?
I spent last week up in the Pacific talking with the Fijian Prime Minister, Mr Rabuka, about regional issues.

What sort of issues?
We've mainly been talking about an aid package.

This is economic aid?
Yes.

And how did it go?
Well, they haven't got a lot. We'll get what we can obviously. I mean, they're only a fairly small country, I don't know that they can answer the entire question.

Thank you very much.
Thank you very much, yourself.

It's always very interesting to talk to you.
It's the least I can do. Have you got any other questions you can ask me? There must be something I should…

What are you going to do about unemployment, Mr Keating?
Well, that's not going to happen until early next year but I thought maybe the speakers' circuit, a bit of gardening…I thought maybe I'd write a book.

I didn't so much mean yours; put it this way, if the Opposition were in government and youth unemployment was thirty-five per cent, what would you be saying?
Any time you want to talk to me about *anything* whatever, you just ring our office…

I appreciate that.
…and I'll just try and make the time to talk to you.

Wouldn't you be saying the Liberal Party never cared about the

working people and that the Labor Party is the one with the heart? The one with the concern for the ordinary people of Australia?

Any time you want to talk to me about *any* issue *whatever*, you just ring the office and I'll make the time to talk to you.

Mr Keating, thanks very much.

Thank *you* very much.

Thanks very much.

Can we shoot this again?

Sure. Why?

I'm not really happy with this tie.

THE AUSTRALIAN OLYMPIC COACH, LIVE FROM BARCELONA

Prospects for the Competition

Live, via satellite, from Barcelona. The coach is wearing a green blazer, yellow shirt and green tie.

Thanks for joining us.
Thank you very much, it's a pleasure.

How's the weather?
Lovely day today. Beautiful day.

And how do you think we'll do?
Well, the swimming people are very pumped up. You'd probably recognise all the usual names, we've got John Dawkins in the backstroke. I think that's Tuesday night.

He's from the Institute, isn't he?
Oh very much so, yes. And with a very unusual style.

What's that?
Well, he swims in the backstroke, but he actually swims feet first; he gets in the water backwards and he kicks off with his head.

And wasn't he having trouble with his turns?
Yes, he doesn't actually do turns, he just swims up to the end,

bumps his head and stops.

What for?
He says he's waiting for someone to turn the pool around.

And what's his best time?
Early afternoon he's probably not bad.

Have you seen anything of John Hewson?
John Hewson and the synchronised swimming team?

Yes.
Yes, they've been training day and night. They're at a bit of a disadvantage unfortunately, over here.

Oh, why's that?
Well, they've noticed that when they dive in, some of the other teams competing over here come up again.

So they've got a bit of work to do?
Unless they can get synchronised drowning recognised as a sport by Thursday it's probably curtains, yes.

And how's Paul Keating doing?
I saw Paul today, he's looking pretty fit, very good. He's in the decathlon of course and quietly confident in all three events.

But the decathlon has ten events.
That's what it says in the program but Paul doesn't agree with the figures.

Gareth Evans looking good?
Gareth Evans isn't actually convinced that the Olympics are on. He thinks it's a press beat-up.

So what's he saying?
Well he's saying that this is the sort of thing that happens from time to time and there's…

…nothing anybody can do about it…

…nothing anybody can do about it, and he's had an incredible response from the Indonesians…

…from the Indonesians, yes. And just finally, how's Bill Kelty doing?

Well Bill's not here yet; unfortunately he seems to have got the venue off a chart in the ACTU office and he hasn't turned up yet. We heard from him today.

Where from?

He's in Helsinki.

Right. So it's gold, gold, gold, eh?

I beg your pardon?

Gold, gold, gold.

No, it's pretty warm here. Lovely day today.

THE AUSTRALIAN OLYMPIC COACH, LIVE FROM BARCELONA

The Position after the First Week

Thanks for joining us.
A pleasure.

Well, it's been a great first week.
Oh marvellous first week, absolutely breathtaking, marvellous first week.

It's a fantastic spectacle isn't it?
It's just the same jacket the rest of the team are wearing, but yes, we get a few comments.

And what's been the highlight so far?
Well, the Australian media are here, I think they've impressed a lot of people.

In what way?
Well they broke the main story of the week, got on to it and nailed it very early. There was a scandal here earlier in the week.

And what was that?
Apparently a lot of the other countries sent swimmers over here.

To Barcelona?

Yes, actually to compete in the swimming events in the Games. A lot of the other countries sent swimmers.

This must have been devastating.

Oh, it's a hell of a thing, a hell of a thing for the team here. A hell of a thing.

And these are *trained* swimmers?

Well, we think so at this stage—they've got to be, they're so fast! Some of these kids are like a knife through…they've impressed our team.

Well how did John Dawkins go, in that case?

John Dawkins went very well, very well indeed. A very commendable performance.

Where did he finish?

I'll let you know when he finishes. He's looking strong at the moment, calling for food.

And how's Paul Keating doing in the decathlon?

He's not in the decathlon any more. He found it conflicted with the dressage, which he wanted to go in, and then he found that you needed a horse for the dressage, and he's now in the rowing.

What event in the rowing?

Single sculls, I would think.

Why did he do that?

He thinks he's more competitive when he can't see where he's going.

And Gareth Evans?

Gareth thinks the whole position here in Barcelona has been exaggerated out of all proportion.

And what's he saying about the fact that the Malaysians took gold in

the badminton?
Oh, he doesn't like the word 'took'.

Why?
He thinks there might be a case that the gold *wanted* to go to Malaysia and he says that this is the type of thing that happens from time to time anyway and …

…there's nothing anybody can do about it…
…there's nothing anybody can do about it…

…and he's had an incredible response from the Indonesians…
…and he's had an incredible response from the Indonesians…

And John Howard?
Yes, the small bore starts on Sunday and we here think he's a bit of a shoo-in. I'd get to the TAB on that one. He's put in a PB every day since he got here.

And has Bill Kelty turned up from Helsinki yet?
No. We've had a couple of planeloads of baggage handlers in today, but no sign of Bill.

And are we still pushing to have dope tests made more comprehensive?
Not until we get John Dawkins out of the water and into the car.

OK. So it's still gold, gold, gold, eh?
I beg your pardon?

Gold, gold, gold?
No, the weather continues beautiful. Gorgeous day today.

**MR BRIAN GREY,
EX-CHIEF EXECUTIVE OF COMPASS
AIRLINES**

Checking the Overhead Locker

Mr Grey, thanks for coming in.
Thank you, it's a pleasure to be here.

The Inquiry by the Securities Commission concerns the rather serious claim that Compass continued to trade after it had run out of money. That's right?
No, that's not right.

That's not right?
No. That's wrong.

That's not what they're saying you did?
No, it *is* what they're *saying* we did.

But you didn't do it?
That's right.

But that's not what they're saying?
That's right too.

I wonder if I could ask you how the airline operated?
Certainly, what we were trying to do was break the stranglehold

held by two internal airlines who simply divided the traffic between them and divided all the money between them. It was about as competitive as a chocolate frog.

What did you do?
When we entered the market we offered the public genuinely cheap airfares. Let's say the cost of flying a passenger from A to B was two hundred dollars. They were charging four hundred dollars.

What did you charge?
We charged a dollar seventy-five.

So you undercut them pretty severely?
We murdered them.

And did the public buy your tickets?
You couldn't get a seat. Our planes were chocka.

What did the other airlines do?
They reduced their fares. We brought about cheap air travel in this country for the first time in history.

By selling something for less than it cost to provide.
Yes, they'd never had to compete with proper business methods before. They didn't know what hit them.

Did they question your methods?
Yes, they tried to white-ant us whenever possible. They couldn't understand it. They said 'Look, the product costs two hundred dollars. How can anyone possibly deliver it for a dollar seventy-five?'

And how did you?
We didn't. It was obviously costing two hundred dollars.

And what were you charging the customer?
A dollar seventy-five.

Where was the rest of the money coming from?
It wasn't coming from anywhere.

So how were you making money?

The planes were full all the time. You couldn't get a seat. We completely revolutionised the domestic air market. I was made Businessman of the Year in 1990.

And what happened?

I have no idea.

What did you do when you realised you were in trouble?

As an airline?

Yes.

We reduced our prices.

Mr Grey, thank you for joining us.

It's a great pleasure. Do you want to share a lottery ticket?

How does that work?

We buy fifteen million dollars' worth of tickets.

And what do we win?

We only win if our number comes up.

What do we win then?

A dollar seventy-five.

THE HON. JOHN HEWSON, LEADER OF THE LIBERAL PARTY

The New Zealand Experiment

Dr Hewson, thanks very much for coming in.
Pleasure.

How are things going?
Pretty well, thanks, yes.

There's been an argument this week about the legitimacy of the Victorian Labor Party's action.
Yes, indeed there has.

In running commercials critical of the Goods and Services Tax in New Zealand.
Yes, I'm familiar with that argument.

Commercials which actually feature New Zealanders disaffected with the Consumption Tax.
Yes. Look, I'm well aware of the argument you're talking about.

People who actually claim to be victims of the sort of system you want to introduce here.
Yes, look, I'm familiar with the matter under discussion.

You don't think it's fair?
It's not supposed to be fair. It's a consumption tax. You take money from everyone and give it back to the people you went to school with.

No, I don't mean the tax being unfair; I meant the use of these commercials by the Victorian Labor Party.
Completely illegitimate. Absolute disgrace.

Why?
Two reasons. Firstly, what's going on in New Zealand is not at issue in an Australian election, and secondly, it isn't true.

What isn't true?
That the Consumption Tax in New Zealand hasn't worked. It HAS worked. It's one of the most spectacularly successful examples of the imposition of a consumption tax in recent economic history.

Is this how you know how you'd implement it here if you got in?
Yes, you can see it in operation.

If it's legitimate for you to go over there and study it and agree with it, why is it illegitimate for someone else to go over there and study it and disagree with it?
Oh, that's a bit unfair isn't it?

Why?
That's a bit below the belt isn't it?

Why?
I've got a feeling it's logical.

If what's going on in New Zealand has no relevance to Australia, why have you been over there studying the Consumption Tax?
What on earth has what's going on in New Zealand got to do with Victoria?

But it's got something to do with Australia?
It will have, yes, we're going to bring it in.

If you get into government?
Yes, we'll bring it in in a big hurry.

Do you think you'll get in?
Yes.

You seem very confident.
Oh yes, New Zealanders can't get the vote over here. I think you'll find we've got that right.

**THE HON. PAUL KEATING,
PRIME MINISTER**

A Policy Vindicated

Mr Keating, thanks for coming in.
Pleasure.

Could you explain the significance of the figures released this week?
Yes, the indications are that we're in recovery, which is completely consistent with government projections, and very gratifying after what I think has been a difficult time for everyone.

It's not a very strong recovery, though, is it?
It's a good recovery, yes. It's driven by private demand, which is what we wanted.

Why did demand increase?
People are having sales. Businesses have dropped their prices to get rid of stock. They've had to. There's a recession on out there, don't you read the papers?

Has inflation gone up?
No, that's what's so fantastic. That's why the recovery has come about.

Why hasn't inflation gone up if demand has gone up?
Because prices haven't gone up. Prices have dropped. That's the only reason there's any demand at all.

And that tends to keep inflation down?
Oh yes.

And this is because of the recession?
Oh yes.

So the cause of the recovery is the recession?
Yes. This is a recession-driven recovery.

That would be pretty unusual, wouldn't it?
We've got scientists coming to Australia to study it. You can't get into a hotel in Canberra.

It does sound unusual.
They said it couldn't be done.

Is it a strong recovery?
No it's not. It's what I would call a weak recovery.

Why is it weak?
It's just being held in check at the moment.

By what?
By the recession.

The recession's not getting any worse, though.
No, it looks a bit like a recovery if you stand in the right position with the light behind it.

How would you describe the recovery?
On the figures available this week, I suppose the recovery is steady without being spectacular.

What does that mean?
It means we're in a recession.

I thought we were over the recession.
Perhaps if we get all the children to hold hands.

Will you be going to assist the Victorian Labor Party in the election campaign?
I'd like to, but unfortunately I can't.

Why not?
Well, we want them to get SOME votes.

**THE HON. NORMAN LAMONT,
CHANCELLOR OF THE EXCHEQUER**

The Currency Crisis

Mr Lamont appears live, via satellite, from London.

Mr Lamont. Thanks for joining us.
Thank you. It's a great pleasure.

We're speaking to you from Australia, of course.
I'll speak as slowly as I can, although I do have to attend a cabinet meeting in about five minutes.

What about?
About my resignation.

So you are actually resigning?
No, I'm not.

Why have a meeting about it then?
Just to get the date of it finalised.

Of your resignation?
Yes indeed.

So you will be resigning?
No, I'll be staying on.

Until when?

Until the meeting. How am I going to determine the date of my resignation if I'm not at the meeting at which it's going to be decided?

Mr Lamont, can you explain the ERM?

I think you'll find it's short for Ernie.

ERM, Mr Lamont.

Or it might be a kind of Greek vase with very attractive handles.

No, the Exchange Rate Mechanism.

Ah. You know something about this. This, of course, was an attempt to link the participating currencies in Western Europe to one another.

A bit of central planning.

No, that's what they did in Eastern Europe. That didn't work at all.

Did this work?

No, you're missing my point. In the Soviet system the value of the currency was set by the governing authority.

Isn't that what you tried to do?

Please don't interrrupt, this is very complex. I'm trying to explain it to you.

Didn't they have a huge black market in the Soviet Union?

Yes. That's exactly what happened. One of the worst problems they had in the Soviet Union was currency speculation.

This is people speculating in the value of other currencies.

Yes, unscrupulous persons motivated by greed and personal gain, with no concern whatever for any damage they might be doing to the economies involved.

We don't have that, of course.

In the West? Good heavens no.

What do we have?
We have the money market, one of the great financial institutions in world history.

And what do they do?
People drop their money off at about 8.30 in the morning and pick it up again at about 5.00 pm.

And what do they do with it?
They buy and sell currencies, establish a pattern of supply and demand and thereby determine price. That's what a market does.

They buy as cheaply as possible and sell for the highest price they can get?
Yes, they buy to optimise their position. That's how the market operates.

Do they care about the economies of the countries involved?
It's a currency market, not a geography lesson.

So, what went wrong?
Well, we're blaming the Germans.

Why?
We're the English. We always blame the Germans.